CW01301587

1 MONTH OF FREE READING

at

www.ForgottenBooks.com

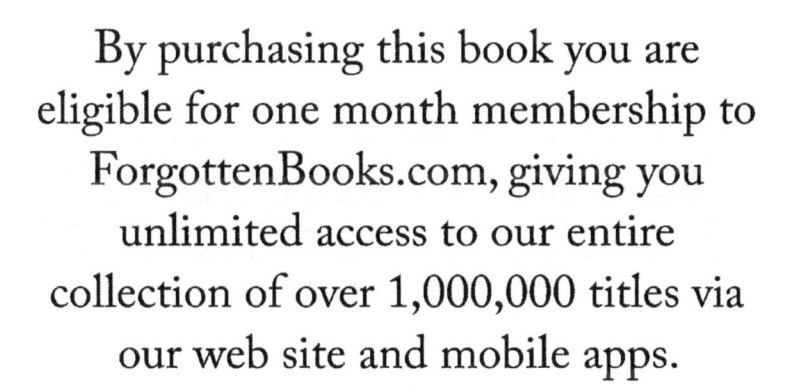

By purchasing this book you are eligible for one month membership to ForgottenBooks.com, giving you unlimited access to our entire collection of over 1,000,000 titles via our web site and mobile apps.

To claim your free month visit: www.forgottenbooks.com/free856121

* Offer is valid for 45 days from date of purchase. Terms and conditions apply.

ISBN 978-0-331-55910-1
PIBN 10856121

This book is a reproduction of an important historical work. Forgotten Books uses state-of-the-art technology to digitally reconstruct the work, preserving the original format whilst repairing imperfections present in the aged copy. In rare cases, an imperfection in the original, such as a blemish or missing page, may be replicated in our edition. We do, however, repair the vast majority of imperfections successfully; any imperfections that remain are intentionally left to preserve the state of such historical works.

Forgotten Books is a registered trademark of FB &c Ltd.
Copyright © 2018 FB &c Ltd.
FB &c Ltd, Dalton House, 60 Windsor Avenue, London, SW19 2RR.
Company number 08720141. Registered in England and Wales.

For support please visit www.forgottenbooks.com

M ICMH
ofiche Collection de
s microfiches
ographs) (monographies)

1995

Technical and Bibliographic Notes / Notes

The Institute has attempted to obtain the best original copy available for filming. Features of this copy which may be bibliographically unique, which may alter any of the images in the reproduction, or which may significantly change the usual method of filming, are checked below.

- [✓] Coloured covers/
  Couverture de couleur

- [ ] Covers damaged/
  Couverture endommagée

- [ ] Covers restored and/or laminated/
  Couverture restaurée et/ou pelliculée

- [ ] Cover title missing/
  Le titre de couverture manque

- [ ] Coloured maps/
  Cartes géographiques en couleur

- [ ] Coloured ink (i.e. other than blue or black)/
  Encre de couleur (i.e. autre que bleue ou noire)

- [ ] Coloured plates and/or illustrations/
  Planches et/ou illustrations en couleur

- [ ] Bound with other material/
  Relié avec d'autres documents

- [ ] Tight binding may cause shadows or distortion along interior margin/
  La reliure serrée peut causer de l'ombre ou de la distorsion le long de la marge intérieure

- [ ] Blank leaves added during restoration may appear within the text. Whenever possible, these have been omitted from filming/
  Il se peut que certaines pages blanches ajoutées lors d'une restauration apparaissent dans le texte, mais, lorsque cela était possible, ces pages n'ont pas été filmées.

- [ ] Additional comments:/
  Commentaires supplémentaires:

L'Institu lui a été

reprodu dans la ci-dessc

- [ ]
- [ ]
- [ ]
- [✓]
- [ ]
- [✓] Tr
- [ ]
- [ ]
- [ ]

Tit
Le

- [ ] Title Page
- [ ]
- [ ]

This item is filmed at the reduction ratio checked below/

ed thanks	L'exemplaire filmé fut reproduit grâce à la générosité de:
	Bibliothèque nationale du Canada
quality gibility the	Les images suivantes ont été reproduites avec le plus grand soin, compte tenu de la condition et de la netteté de l'exemplaire filmé, et en conformité avec les conditions du contrat de filmage.
re filmed ng on Impres- . All g on the pres- printed	Les exemplaires originaux dont la couverture en papier est imprimée sont filmés en commençant par le premier plat et en terminant soit par la dernière page qui comporte une empreinte d'impression ou d'illustration, soit par le second plat, selon le cas. Tous les autres exemplaires originaux sont filmés en commençant par la première page qui comporte une empreinte d'impression ou d'illustration et en terminant par la dernière page qui comporte une telle empreinte.
"CON- END"),	Un des symboles suivants apparaîtra sur la dernière image de chaque microfiche, selon le cas: le symbole —▶ signifie "A SUIVRE", le symbole ▽ signifie "FIN".
at to be ed left to as the	Les cartes, planches, tableaux, etc., peuvent être filmés à des taux de réduction différents. Lorsque le document est trop grand pour être reproduit en un seul cliché, il est filmé à partir de l'angle supérieur gauche, de gauche à droite, et de haut en bas, en prenant le nombre d'images nécessaire. Les diagrammes suivants illustrent la méthode.

1
2
3

MICROCOPY RESOLUTION TEST CHART

(ANSI and ISO TEST CHART No. 2)

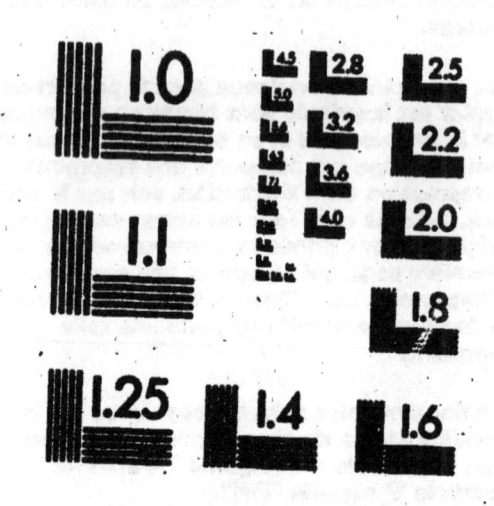

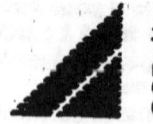

APPLIED IMAGE Inc
1653 East Main Street
Rochester, New York 14609 USA
(716) 482-0300 - Phone
(716) 288-5989 - Fax

Morang's Literature Series

Macaulay's
Lays of
Ancient Rome

1. **High School Poetry Book, Part I.** Edited with notes by W. J. Sykes, B.A., English Specialist, Collegiate Institute, Ottawa.

2. **High School Poetry Book, Part II.** Edited with notes by W. J. Sykes, B.A.

3. **Poems of the Love of Country.** Edited with notes by J. E. Wetherell, B.A., Inspector of High Schools for Ontario.

4. **Selections from Tennyson.** Edited with notes by John C. Saul, M.A.

5. **High School Ballad Book.** Edited with notes by F. F. Macpherson, B.A., Assistant Master, Normal School, Hamilton.

6. **Modern English Ballads.** Edited with notes by F. F. Macpherson, B.A. *In preparation.*

7. **Selections from the Nature Poets.** Edited with notes by Andrew Stevenson, B.A., Assistant Master, Normal School, London.

8. **Selections from the Canadian Prose Writers.** Edited with notes by E. A. Hardy, B.A., formerly Principal, Moulton College, Toronto. *In preparation.*

9. **Selections from the Canadian Poets.** Edited with notes by E. A. Hardy, B.A.

10. **Selections from Wordsworth.** Edited with notes by Alexander Mowat, B.A., Inspector of Public Schools, Peter-

11. **Selections from Byron, Shelly and Keats.** Edited with notes by S. J. Radcliffe, B.A., Principal, Normal School, London. *In preparation.*

12. **High School Poetry Book, Part III.** Edited with notes by John C. Saul, M.A.

13. **High School Prose Book, Part I.** Edited with notes by O. J. Stevenson, M.A., D.Pæd., Professor of Pedagogy, Queen's University, Kingston.

16. **Narrative Poems.** Edited with notes by John C. Saul, M.A.
17. **Hawthorne's Wonder Book.** Edited with notes by John C. Saul, M.A.
18. **Selections from Longfellow.** Edited with notes by John C. Saul, M.A.
19. **Hawthorne's Tanglewood Tales.** Edited with notes by John C. Saul, M.A.
20. **Shakespeare's Merchant of Venice.** Edited with notes by Miss Gertrude Lawler, M.A., English Specialist, Harbord Collegiate Institute, Toronto.
21. **Shakespeare's Julius Cæsar.** Edited with notes by F. C. Colbeck, B.A., Principal, Humberside Collegiate Institute, Toronto.
22. **Shakespeare's As You Like It.** Edited with notes by J. F. Van Every, B.A., English Specialist, Collegiate Institute, Owen Sound.
23. **Shakespeare's Macbeth.** Edited with notes by Miss A. E. Allin, M.A., formerly English Specialist, High School, Lindsay.
24. **Public School Poetry Book, Part I.** Edited with notes by J. F. White, B.A., LL.D., Principal, Provincial Normal School, Ottawa, and W. J. Sykes, B.A.
25. **Public School Poetry Book, Part II.** Edited with notes by J. F. White, B.A., LL.D., and W. J. Sykes, B.A.
26. **Public School Poetry Book, Part III.** Edited with notes by J. F. White, B.A., LL.D., and W. J. Sykes, B.A.
27. **Scott's, The Lay of the Last Minstrel.** Edited with notes by John C. Saul, M.A.
28. **High School Reading Book.**
29. **Longer Narrative Poems.** Edited with notes by John Jeffries, B.A., English Specialist, Jarvis Collegiate Institute, Toronto.

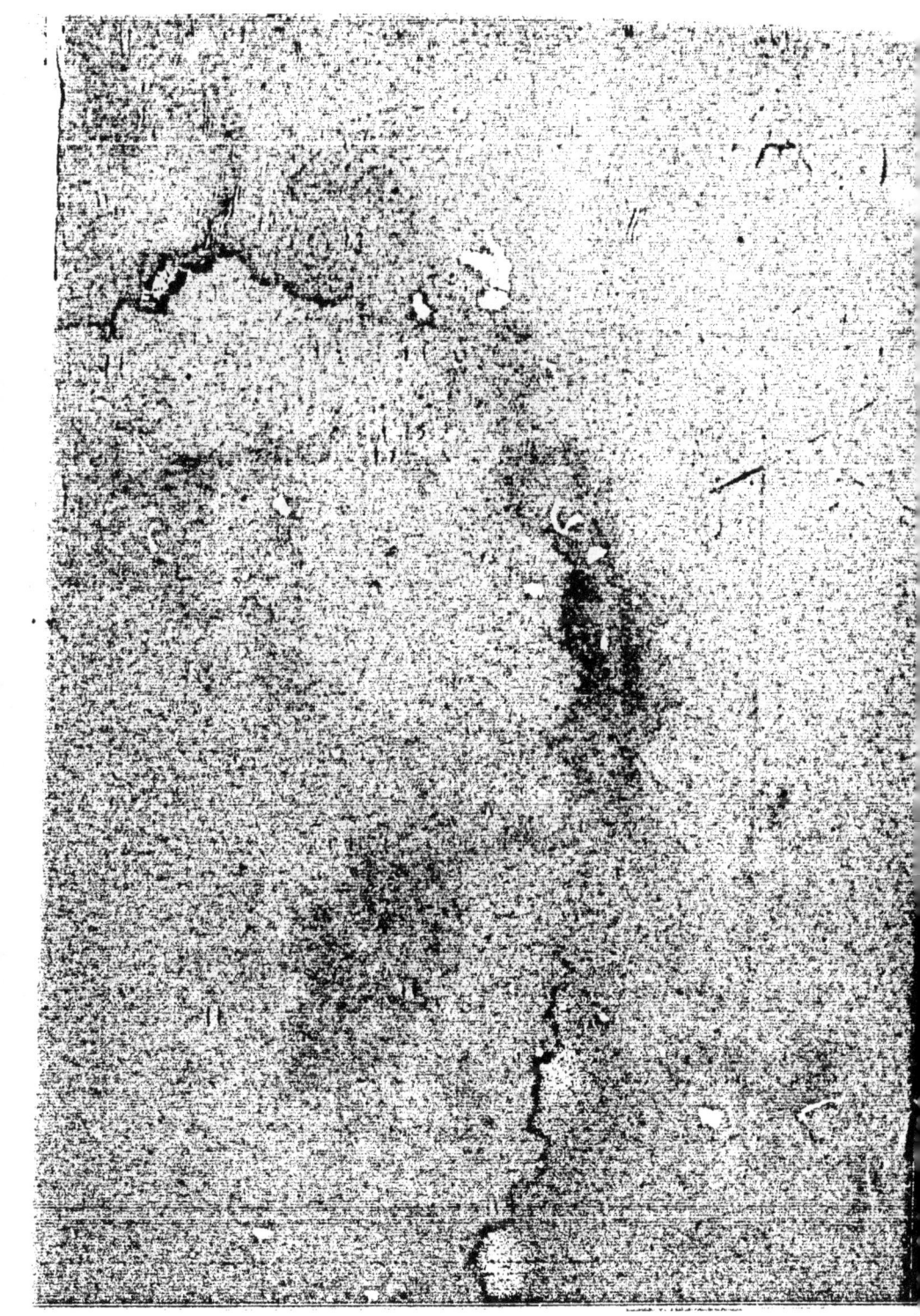

THE COUNTRIES OF ANCIENT ITALY

MORANG'S LITERATURE SERIES

MACAULAY'S

LAYS OF ANCIENT ROME

EDITED WITH NOTES

BY

JOHN C. SAUL, M.A.

WINNIPEG
CLARK BROS. & CO., LIMITED
TORONTO
MORANG EDUCATIONAL COMPANY LIMITED
1910

1910

Copyright, Canada, 1910, by
MORANG EDUCATIONAL COMPANY LIMITED

NOTE

THE editor desires to acknowledge his indebtedness to Rolfe's edition of the *Lays of Ancient Rome*, to Liddell's *History of Rome*, and to Haaren and Poland's *Famous Men of Rome*, all three books published by the American Book Company. The illustrations in the text are from the *Ontario High School Ancient History*.

MAP OF ROME
During the Early Days of the Republic

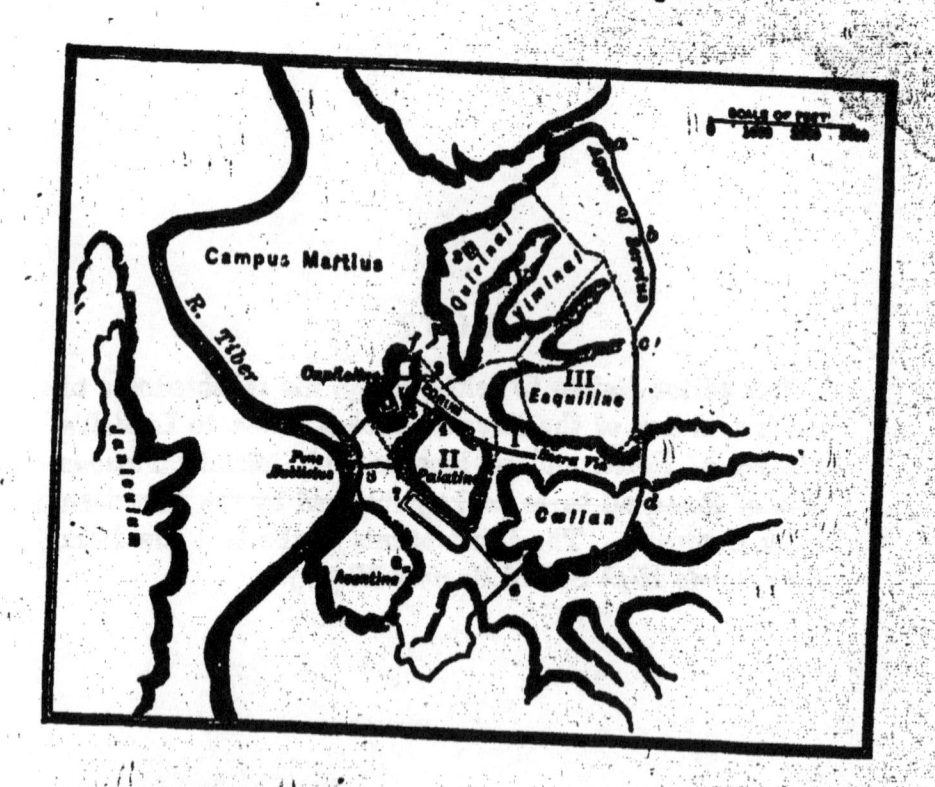

The four Servian regions: I., Suburana; II., Palatina; III., Esquilina; IV., Collina.

The chief gates of Rome: a, Collina; b, Viminalis; c, Esquilian; d, Querquetulana; e, Capena; f, Ratumena.

The chief buildings, etc.: 1, Temple of Jupiter Capitolinus; 2, Janus; 3, Quirinus; 4, Vesta; 5, Saturn; 6, Diana; 7, Circus Maximus; 8, Cloaca Maxima; 9, Vicus Tuscus.

CONTENTS

GENERAL INTRODUCTION	9
Life of Macaulay	9
The Lays of Ancient Rome	11
HORATIUS	13
THE BATTLE OF THE LAKE REGILLUS	49
VIRGINIA	87
THE PROPHECY OF CAPYS	115

THE ENVIRONS OF ROME

GENERAL INTRODUCTION

LIFE OF MACAULAY

THOMAS BABINGTON MACAULAY was born at Rothley Temple, Leicestershire, England, on the 25th of October, 1800. He was the son of Zachary Macaulay, a merchant engaged in the African trade, but more interested in the movement for the abolition of slavery, of which he was one of the foremost advocates. The young Macaulay was a marvellously gifted child, and early showed the strong literary bent of his mind. Before he was eight years of age he had written a *Compendium of Universal History*, and a vast quantity of poetry, both in rhyme and in blank verse. These literary exercises, however, did not do the child any harm, nor did they interfere in any way with his regular school work. He was educated for a time at home, but at the age of twelve he was placed in a private school, where he made such surprising progress that in 1818 he went into residence at Trinity College, Cambridge. During his college course he gained on two occasions the Chancellor's medal for poetry, and greatly distinguished himself as a debater and conversationalist. His dislike for mathematics, however, prevented him from taking high honors. He took his degree of Master of Arts in 1825, and in 1826 was called to the bar. He practised law for about two years, but was not successful, and finally abandoned his profession altogether.

As early as 1824 Macaulay had made his appearance as a public speaker at an anti-slavery meeting, winning high praise for his speech on that occasion. He made his first appearance in print in Knight's *Quarterly Magazine*, but it was not until 1825, when he published his celebrated article on Milton in the *Edinburgh Review*, that he acquired the reputation for literary skill and critical ability that remained with him all his life. His connection with the *Edinburgh Review* continued for over twenty years, and in its pages were published the most brilliant products of his pen. Macaulay was now recognized as a powerful speaker and writer. The doors of society were opened to him; he became the companion and intimate of some of the most distinguished men and women of the day.

In 1828 Zachary Macaulay failed in business, and the support of the family fell largely upon his son. This was the most trying period of Macaulay's life. At one time he was reduced to such straits that he was compelled to sell his college prizes. In 1828 he was made a Commissioner of Bankruptcy, but this office was abolished in 1830. But through all his troubles and reverses he kept a smiling face and a cheerful heart, and never allowed those dependent upon him to suspect that he felt the hardness of the struggle. In the end he triumphed over all difficulties.

In 1830 Macaulay took his seat in the House of Commons as member for Calne, a pocket-borough in the gift of Lord Lansdowne, who was an admirer of his literary gifts. He soon leaped to the front as one of the first Parliamentary debaters of his time. He took an active part in the passage of the Reform Bill, and made several powerful speeches in 'ts support. In 1832 he was appointed one of the Commissioners of the Board of Control of Indian Affairs, and gave his attention to the study of problems affecting the government of India. In 1833, in the first Parliament under the

Reform Bill, he sat as one of the members for Leeds, but resigned in the next year to accept a seat in the Supreme Council of India at a salary of £10,000 a year. He remained in India for four years, when he returned to England, and again entered Parliament as a representative for Edinburgh. In 1839 he became Secretary of War with a seat in the Cabinet, but held office for only two years, retiring on the fall of the Melbourne ministry. In 1846 he resumed office as Paymaster-General. In the next year, however, he lost his seat for Edinburgh, owing to the stand he had taken in connection with Irish educational affairs, and retired to private life.

Macaulay did not regret his enforced retirement from public office. He now had leisure to devote to his life work, the *History of England,* the first two volumes of which appeared in 1848. In 1849 he was chosen Lord Rector of the University of Glasgow, and in 1852 his former constituency of Edinburgh returned him at the head of the poll, although he did not solicit the nomination, nor did he take any part in the campaign or visit the city during the election. In 1857 he was raised to the peerage as Lord Macaulay of Rothley. He died at Kensington on the 25th of December, 1859, and was buried in Westminster Abbey.

The *History of England,* great though it is, is a mere fragment, as Macaulay did not live to carry out the plan that he had formed. Volumes 3 and 4 were published in 1855, and Volume 5 was incomplete at the time of his death. His other writings are *Essays* and the *Lays of Ancient Rome.*

THE LAYS OF ANCIENT ROME

Macaulay takes for granted that what is called the history of the kings and consuls of Rome is to a large extent fabulous. He supposes that a literature, older than any now preserved, existed in Rome, and that this literature was a product of the people and written in the form of ballads. He further supposes that these forgotten ballads were the sources from which the Annalists, who later compiled the history of Rome, drew their material. The *Lays of Ancient Rome* is an attempt to reproduce some of these ancient ballads.

In his Introduction, Macaulay says: "In the following poems the author speaks, not in his own person, but in the persons of ancient minstrels who know only what a Roman citizen, born three or four hundred years before the Christian era, may be supposed to have known, and who are in no wise above the passions and prejudices of their age and nation. To these imaginary poets must be ascribed some blunders, which are so obvious that it is unnecessary to point them out. The real blunder would have been to represent these old poets as deeply versed in general history, and studious of chronological accuracy. To them must also be attributed the illiberal sneers at the Greeks, the furious party spirit, the contempt for the arts of peace, the love of war for its own sake, the ungenerous exultation over the vanquished which the reader will sometimes observe. To portray a Roman of the age of Camillus or Curius as superior to national antipathies, as mourning over the devastation and slaughter by which empire and triumphs were to be won, as looking on human suffering with the sympathy of Howard, or as treating conquered enemies with the delicacy of the Black Prince, would be to violate all dramatic propriety. The old Romans had some great virtues, — fortitude, temperance, veracity, spirit to resist oppression, respect for legitimate authority, fidelity in the observing of contracts, disinterestedness, ardent patriotism; but Christian charity and chivalrous generosity were alike unknown to them."

INTRODUCTION
TO
HORATIUS

THE first king of Rome was Romulus, the founder of the city. After him six kings ruled in succession, the last being Lucius Tarquinius, surnamed *Superbus*, or the Proud, on account of his haughty disposition. On the death of the fifth king, Tarquinius Priscus, Servius Tullius succeeded to the throne, and reigned for forty-four years. Tarquinius Priscus, however, had left two sons, Lucius and Aruns, and Servius, fearing that they might conspire against him, had married them to his two daughters. His eldest daughter was given in marriage to Lucius, who was bold and ambitious, while the younger sister was wedded to Aruns, the gentler and quieter of the two brothers. But Tullia was also bold and ambitious, and she and Lucius soon conspired to seize the throne. Lucius murdered his wife, Tullia her husband, and the two were married. Shortly afterwards they caused the death of Servius, and Lucius, with the aid of the nobles who were angered at the favor shown to the common people, had himself proclaimed king.

The noble families who had helped Tarquin in his plans soon had reason to regret their action. Tarquin, it is true, oppressed the common people by loading them with taxes and by compelling them to work without pay on the roads and public buildings, but at the same time he reduced the power of the nobles and deprived them of many of their privileges. All who opposed him were put to death or banished from the city. Both nobles and common people were soon anxious to get rid of the tyrant. Tarquin, however, strengthened his position by forming alliances with neighboring kings and peoples, especially with the Etruscan and Latin cities, so that he became daily stronger and more absolute. The citizens were compelled to submit, as they did not feel themselves strong enough to oppose successfully their tyrant king.

Tarquin had in various ways succeeded in making himself the head of the confederacy of Latin cities, but Gabii, an important stronghold, held out against him. The city was finally won through an act of the basest treachery on the part of Sextus, the youngest son of the king. Sextus fled to Gabii, and there begged for refuge, saying that he had been driven from Rome by the cruelty of his father. The people of Gabii believed him, and in time he became the leader of their armies. Tarquin allowed his son to win some unimportant victories over the Romans, and this increased the confidence of the Gabians in their general. When Sextus felt himself secure in his position, he made false charges against leading citizens, and had many of them banished and others put to death. In a short time there was no one strong enough to oppose him, and he surrendered the city to his father. The possession of Gabii made Tarquin the undisputed master of the Latin League. Although it was Sextus who had brought about this result, yet it was this same Sextus who was the means of ruining the Tarquins and causing their banishment from Rome.

Tarquin, in his efforts to strengthen his power, did not spare even the members of his own family. He was jealous of his sister's sons and put the elder to death, but allowed the younger, Lucius Junius, to live, as he did not think him capable of doing any harm. In reality Lucius was a very able man, but feigned stupidity in order to deceive his uncle and to save his own life. So successful was he that he imposed upon not only his uncle, but also upon all the people, and gained for himself the surname of Brutus, or the Dullard. He was waiting the opportunity to serve his country by driving Tarquin from the throne.

Among the most important public works undertaken by Tarquin was the erection of a temple on the Capitoline Hill, in honor of the three great divinities, Jupiter, Juno, and Minerva. While the temple was being constructed, an unusual incident occurred. As a sacrifice was being offered to the gods, a snake appeared and devoured the animal that was being burned on the altar. Tarquin could not understand what this marvel might mean, and sent his two sons, Aruns and Titus, accompanied by Brutus, to consult the famous oracle of the god Apollo, at Delphi, in Greece. The answer was not satisfactory, but the young men were curious and asked many questions. Among others they asked who should rule after Tarquin. The answer was, "Whichever of you three young men shall first kiss your mother shall be the next ruler of Rome." Titus and Aruns at once set out for Rome, each eager to be the first to kiss his mother; but Brutus, with a clearer idea of what the oracle really meant, as soon as he landed in Italy, fell to the ground and kissed the earth, the mother of us all.

When Titus, Aruns, and Brutus returned home, they at once joined the army that was besieging Ardea, one of the cities with which Rome was then at war. One night, during a feast at which Collatinus, who was the cousin of Tarquin and the governor of Collatia, was present, a dispute arose among the young men as to the wife of which of them should be held in the highest esteem. Collatinus proposed that they should visit their homes in a body that evening, and find out how their wives were occupying their time. The proposal was accepted, and the house of each was visited in turn. At Rome they found the princesses enjoying a splendid banquet, but at the home of Collatinus, in Collatia, they found his beautiful wife, Lucretia, with her maidens round her, engaged in spinning wool for the household use. All agreed in awarding the highest honor to Lucretia.

Soon after this visit Sextus Tarquin deeply injured Lucretia, who sent at once for her husband, Collatinus, and for her father, Spurius Lucretius, who was governor of Rome in the absence of the king. Collatinus brought with him Brutus, and Lucretius came accompanied by Publius Valerius. Lucretia told them of the bitter wrong that had been done her, and after pledging them to avenge her, stabbed herself to the heart. Brutus, who now threw off his mask of stupidity, plucked the dagger from her breast, and holding it up, exclaimed, "By this pure blood I swear before the gods that I will pursue Lucius Tarquinius, the Proud, and all his bloody house with fire, sword, or in whatsoever way I may, and that neither they nor any other shall hereafter be king of Rome." The body was then carried into the Forum of Collatia, where Brutus told the story to the citizens, and called on them to rid the Roman dominions of the Tarquins. The people of Collatia rose at once, and Brutus led them to Rome. Here Brutus told the story again and urged the citizens to join him in avenging the injury done to the dead Lucretia. His appeal was answered. The citizens armed themselves and closed the gates of the city.

As soon as Tarquin heard of the revolt, he hastened to Rome, on the way crossing Brutus, who was hurrying to Ardea. The army, as soon as they heard the story, placed themselves under the command of Brutus, drove out the sons of Tarquin, and marched to Rome. In the meantime, Tarquin had reached the city, but was refused admittance. There was nothing for the king and his sons but to take refuge with their friends and allies outside of Rome.

The Romans now made up their minds to have no more kings, but instead they elected two chief magistrates, who were afterwards known as Consuls. The Consuls were elected each year by the whole body of the people, and, during their year of office, they held almost kingly power. The choice of the people at the first election fell on Brutus and on Collatinus, the husband of Lucretia. Collatinus, however, was soon compelled to resign, as he had been too closely related to the Tarquins in their days of power; and Publius Valerius, surnamed Poplicola, or "the friend of the people," was elected in his place.

But the Tarquins in their exile were not idle. Messengers who came to Rome to demand the return of the private property of the king succeeded in forming a conspiracy among a number of the young nobles who were favorable to the exiled house. A slave chanced to hear the conspirators arranging their plans, and betrayed the plot to Brutus. The messengers were arrested, and letters were found on them which implicated a large number of young Romans. Among those who had signed the letters were Titus and Tiberius, the sons of Brutus. The stern Consul would not listen to any appeals for mercy, and had his two sons executed in his presence, the first of all the plotters. This was the first attempt of the Tarquins to regain their power.

When Tarquin saw that the plot within the city had

failed, he persuaded the people of Tarquinii and Veii to come to his assistance, and to make war on the Romans. Brutus led the Roman cavalry, and was opposed to Aruns, the son of Tarquin, who commanded the cavalry of the enemy. When Aruns saw Brutus, he rushed at him, and in the single combat that followed both leaders were killed. The result of the battle was in doubt, but in the night a mysterious voice proclaimed that the Romans were victorious, as they had lost one man less than their opponents. The enemy fled in the night, and thus the second attempt of Tarquin to regain his throne ended in failure.

ROMAN FARMER PLOWING

Tarquin now turned for assistance to Lars Porsena, king of Clusium. Porsena was at the head of the Etruscan League, a confederacy of the twelve great cities of Etruria, and he soon had gathered a powerful army with which to compel the Romans to submission. The story of his unsuccessful attempt to surprise the city is told in *Horatius*. After the destruction of the bridge, Porsena laid siege to Rome, and refused to make peace unless the Tarquins were restored. But the Romans held out bravely, and, in spite of famine and disease, for a long time refused to surrender. Finally they were compelled to admit Porsena into the city, and to acknowledge him as master. They agreed to give up all the lands they had won from the Etruscans, and to furnish hostages, as a pledge that they would carry out their promises to the Etruscans. Porsena, however, did not insist on the restoration of Tarquin. The third attempt of the Tarquins was thus unsuccessful. The story of the fourth and last attempt is told in *The Battle of the Lake Regillus.*

Macaulay in his Introduction says: "The following ballad is supposed to have been made about a hundred and twenty years after the war which it celebrates, and just before the taking of Rome by the Gauls. The author seems to have been an honest citizen, proud of the military glory of his country, sick of the disputes of factions, and much given to pining after good old times which had never really existed. The allusion, however, to the partial manner in which the public lands were allotted could proceed only from a plebeian; and the allusion to the fraudulent sale of spoils marks the date of the poem, and shows that the poet shared in the general discontent with which the proceedings of Camillus, after the taking of Veii, were regarded."

Professor Henry Morley, in speaking of the mythical character of the story of Horatius, says: "In the first of these *Lays,* the old Roman story of three Romans who saved Rome by keeping the bridge over the Tiber against all the force of Porsena, was the ingenious softening of a cruel fact. It turned a day of deep humiliation into the bright semblance of a day of glory. For we learn from Tacitus and others that Porsena became absolute master of Rome. The Senate of Rome paid homage to him with offering of an ivory throne, a crown, a sceptre, a triumphal robe; and he forbade the use of iron by the Romans in forging weapons or armor. The happy time of release from thraldom was long celebrated by a custom of opening auctions with a first bid for 'the goods of Porsena.' What did this matter? The songs of the people were free to suppress a great defeat, and put in its place the myth of a heroic deed; some small fact usually serving as seed that shall grow and blossom out into a noble tale. A ballad-maker who should stop the course of a popular legend to investigate its origin, and who should be dull enough to include that investigation in his song, would deserve to be howled to death by the united voices of his countrymen."

HORATIUS

A LAY MADE ABOUT THE YEAR OF THE CITY[1] CCCLX

1

Lars Porsena[2] of Clusium[3]
  By the Nine Gods[4] he swore
That the great house of Tarquin
  Should suffer wrong no more.
By the Nine Gods he swore it,
  And named a trysting day,[5]
And bade his messengers ride forth
East and west and south and north,
  To summon his array.

2

East and west and south and north
  The messengers ride fast,
And tower and town and cottage
  Have heard the trumpet's blast.

---

[1] *Year of the city.* The city of Rome is supposed to have been founded 753 B.C. This would make the date of the poem 393 B.C.

[2] *Lars Porsena.* The honorary title *Lars* usually was given to the Etruscan kings. It is supposed to mean "king."

[3] *Clusium.* The city of Clusium, now known as Chiusi, was situated on the river Clanis, a tributary of the Tiber, about eighty miles from Rome.

[4] *Nine Gods.* Only nine of the gods of the Etruscans had control over the thunder; hence they were recognised as the chief divinities.

[5] *Trysting day.* A place and time at which the armies should meet.

Shame on the false Etruscan
  Who lingers in his home,
When Porsena of Clusium
  Is on the march for Rome.

3

The horsemen and the footmen
  Are pouring in amain [1]
From many a stately market-place;
  From many a fruitful plain;
From many a lonely hamlet,
  Which, hid by beech and pine,
Like an eagle's nest, hangs on the crest
  Of purple Apennine;

4

From lordly Volaterræ,[2]
  Where scowls the far-famed hold
Piled by the hands of giants
  For godlike kings of old;
From sea-girt Populonia,[3]
  Whose sentinels descry
Sardinia's snowy mountain-tops
  Fringing the southern sky;

---

[1] *Amain.* With the utmost speed.

[2] *Volaterræ.* An almost impregnable fortress, situated on the top of a steep mountain 1700 feet high, about five miles from the river Cæcina, and fifteen miles from the sea-coast. The ruins show that the walls were built of huge blocks of stone fitted together without mortar. Parts of the walls still standing are forty feet high and thirteen feet thick.

[3] *Populonia.* One of the Etruscan cities situated on a lofty hill near the sea-shore. Strabo, the Greek geographer, says that the mountains of Sardinia are visible from Populonia, but this is impossible, as the nearer mountains of Elba cut off the view.

5

From the proud mart of Pisæ,[1]
35   Queen of the western waves,
Where ride Massilia's triremes [2]
    Heavy with fair-haired slaves;
From where sweet Clanis [3] wanders
    Through corn and vines and flowers;
40   From where Cortona [4] lifts to heaven
    Her diadem of towers.

6

Tall are the oaks whose acorns
    Drop in dark Auser's rill;[5]
Fat are the stags that champ the boughs
45   Of the Ciminian hill;[6]

---

[1] *Pisæ.* One of the Etruscan cities situated on the north bank of the river Arno, a few miles from its mouth. The modern city of Pisa now occupies the ancient site.

[2] *Massilia's triremes.* Massilia is the modern Marseilles. It was founded by the Phœnicians about 600 B.C., and was an important commercial centre. *Triremes* were ships with three banks of oars. The slaves were principally *fair-haired* Gauls obtained from the interior of France and from Germany.

[3] *Clanis.* Now known as the Chiana, a tributary of the river Tiber.

[4] *Cortona.* One of the Etruscan cities situated on the top of a mountain about nine miles from Lake Trasimenus. The ruins of the ancient walls are still standing.

[5] *Auser's rill.* The Auser is a river of Etruria, a tributary of the river Tiber.

Beyond all streams Clitumnus [1]
  Is to the herdsman dear;
Best of all pools the fowler loves
  The great Volsinian mere.[2]

7

50 But now no stroke of woodman
  Is heard by Auser's rill;
No hunter tracks the stag's green path
  Up the Ciminian hill;
Unwatched along Clitumnus
55   Grazes the milk-white steer;
Unharmed the water fowl may dip
  In the Volsinian mere.

8

The harvests of Arretium,[3]
  This year, old men shall reap,
60 This year, young boys in Umbro [4]
  Shall plunge the struggling sheep;
And in the vats of Luna,[5]
  This year, the must [6] shall foam

---

[1] *Clitumnus.* The region through which the Clitumnus flowed, on its way to the Tiber, was celebrated for a peculiar breed of cattle. Their *milk-whiteness* was supposed to be due to their drinking from the clear waters of the stream.

[2] *Volsinian mere.* A lake, or mere, in Etruria, about sixty miles from Rome. It took its name from the town of Volsinii situated on its banks. Part of the lake was swampy and filled with reeds.

[3] *Arretium.* One of the Etruscan cities, now known as Arezzo, situated in the valley of the Arno, about four miles south of the river. The district surrounding the city was very fertile.

[4] *Umbro.* A river of Etruria, now the Ombrone, flowing into the sea south of the Arno.

[5] *Luna.* An Etruscan city, celebrated for its wine, situated near the mouth of the river Macra.

[6] *Must.* New wine, or unfermented grape-juice.

> There be thirty chosen prophets,
>   The wisest of the land,
> Who alway by Lars Porsena
>   Both morn and evening stand:
> 70 Evening and morn the Thirty
>   Have turned the verses [1] o'er,
> Traced from the right [2] on linen white
>   By mighty seers of yore.
>
> 10
>
> And with one voice the Thirty
> 75   Have their glad answer given:
> "Go forth, go forth, Lars Porsena;
>   Go forth, beloved of Heaven:
> Go, and return in glory
>   To Clusium's royal dome;
> 80 And hang round Nurscia's altars [3]
>   The golden shields [4] of Rome."

---

[1] *Verses.* The ancient, sacred prophetic books, written on white linen specially prepared for the purpose.

[2] *From the right.* Written from right to left, as is the case with the Hebrew and other languages.

[3] *Nurscia's altars.* Nurscia was the Etruscan goddess of fortune. A magnificent temple was erected in her honor at Volsinii.

[4] *Golden shields.* During the reign of one of the early Roman kings, Numa Pompilius, while a pestilence was threatening to destroy the city, a golden shield is said to have fallen from heaven, as a sign of the favor of the gods. As the fate of Rome was believed to depend upon the preservation of this shield, Numa caused eleven others to be prepared exactly like it, so that the danger of losing the genuine one might be lessened. The shields, or *ancilia*, were kept in the temple of

85   And now hath every city
          Sent up her tale [1] of men :
      The foot are fourscore thousand,
          The horse are thousands ten.
      Before the gates of Sutrium [2]
          Is met the great array.
      A proud man was Lars Porsena
          Upon the trysting day.

12

90   For all the Etruscan armies
          Were ranged beneath his eye,
      And many a banished Roman,
          And many a stout ally;
      And with a mighty following
95   To join the muster came
      The Tusculan Mamilius,[3]
          Prince of the Latian name.

---

the goddess Vesta, and a special order of priests, the *Salii*, twelve in number, was appointed to guard them. On the 1st of March in each year the shields were carried in procession around the city, accompanied by the priests dancing and singing in praise of Mars, the god of war. During the three days that the festival lasted all business was suspended in Rome.

[1] *Tale.* Number.

[2] *Sutrium.* A small Etruscan city, now known as Sutri, situated on a hill about thirty-two miles from Rome.

[3] *Mamilius.* Octavius Mamilius, a member of one of the most distinguished families of Tusculum, had married the daughter of Tarquin. He took up the quarrel of his father-in-law, and led the Latin allies of Porsena. Tusculum was a very strong city, now known as Frascati, upon a spur of the Alban Hills, about fifteen miles from Rome.

13

    But by the yellow Tiber [1]
        Was tumult and affright:
100 From all the spacious champaign [2]
        To Rome men took their flight.
    A mile around the city,
        The throng stopped up the ways;
    A fearful sight it was to see
105   Through two long nights and days.

14

    For aged folks on crutches,
        And women great with child,
    And mothers sobbing over babes
        That clung to them and smiled.
110 And sick men borne in litters
        High on the necks of slaves,
    And troops of sun-burned husbandmen
        With reaping-hooks and staves,

15

    And droves of mules and asses
115   Laden with skins of wine, [3]
    And endless flocks of goats and sheep,
        And endless herds of kine,
    And endless trains of wagons
        That creaked beneath the weight
120 Of corn-sacks and of household goods,
        Choked every roaring gate.

---

[1] *Yellow Tiber.* Probably so called from the reddish yellow soil at the bottom of the river.

[2] *Champaign.* Open country.

16

Now, from the rock Tarpeian,[1]
  Could the wan burghers[2] spy
The line of blazing villages
  Red in the midnight sky.
The Fathers of the City,[3]
  They sat all night and day,
For every hour some horseman came
  With tidings of dismay.

17

To eastward and to westward
  Have spread the Tuscan bands;
Nor house nor fence nor dovecote
  In Crustumerium[4] stands.
Verbenna down to Ostia[5]
  Hath wasted all the plain;

---

[1] *Rock Tarpeian.* In the early days of Rome while the Sabines were besieging the city, Tarpeia, the daughter of the governor of the citadel, offered to open the gates, provided the Sabines would give her "that which they wore on their left arms," meaning their gold bracelets. The offer was accepted, and Tarpeia opened the gates. As the Sabines entered, their leader threw not only his bracelets, but his shield which he also wore on his left arm, over Tarpeia, and his men following his example, she was crushed to death. She was buried where she fell, and the rock was from that time known by her name. Traitors were in after days hurled to their death from this rock.

[2] *Burghers.* Citizens.

[3] *Fathers of the City.* The Patres Conscripti, or *enrolled fathers*, were the members of the Senate, the governing body of Rome. At this time the Senate numbered three hundred members.

[4] *Crustumerium.* One of the Latin cities near Rome.

[5] *Ostia.* The seaport of Rome, at the mouth of the Tiber, about sixteen miles from the city. The site of the ancient town is now three miles inland.

Forthwith up rose the Consul,[3]
Up rose the Fathers all;
In haste they girded up their gowns,[4]
145   And hied them to the wall.

19

They held a council standing
Before the River-Gate;[5]
Short time was there, ye well may guess,
For musing or debate.
150   Out spake the Consul roundly:
"The bridge[6] must straight go down;

---

[1] *Janiculum.* A hill across the Tiber from Rome, with which it was connected by a bridge. One of the early kings of Rome had erected a strong fortress on the top of the hill, as a protection against the Etruscans. See Map, page 6.

[2] *Iwis.* An adverb meaning "certainly" or "assuredly." The word was originally written *ywis*.

[3] *Consul.* After the expulsion of the kings, the chief officers of the Roman state, two in number and elected annually, were termed Consuls. See Introduction, page 17.

[4] *Gowns.* The outer garment, or *toga*, of the Romans was a long robe of white wool.

[5] *River-Gate.* The Porta Flumentana, opposite Janiculum. See Map, page 6.

[6] *The bridge.* The Pons Sublicius, a wooden bridge which connected

For, since Janiculum is lost,
　　Naught else can save the town."

20

Just then a scout came flying,
　　All wild with haste and fear;
"To arms! to arms! Sir Consul:
　Lars Porsena is here."
On the low hills to westward
　　The Consul fixed his eye,
And saw the swarthy storm of dust
　　Rise fast along the sky.

21

And nearer fast and nearer
　　Doth the red whirlwind come;
And louder still and still more loud,
From underneath that rolling cloud,
Is heard the trumpet's war-note proud,
　　The trampling, and the hum.
And plainly and more plainly
　　Now through the gloom appears,
Far to left and far to right,
In broken gleams of dark-blue light,
The long array of helmets bright,
　　The long array of spears.

22

And plainly and more plainly
　　Above that glimmering line,
Now might ye see the banners
　　Of twelve fair cities [1] shine:

---

[1] *Twelve fair cities.* The Etruscan confederacy was composed of twelve cities.

But the banner of proud Clusium
　　Was highest of them all,
180　The terror of the Umbrian,[1]
　　The terror of the Gaul.[2]

23

And plainly and more plainly
　　Now might the burghers know,
By port and vest,[3] by horse and crest,
185　Each warlike Lucumo.[4]
There Cilnius of Arretium
　　On his fleet roan was seen;
And Astur of the fourfold shield,[5]
Girt with the brand[6] none else may wield,
190　Tolumnius with the belt of gold,
And dark Verbenna from the hold
　　By reedy Thrasymene.[7]

24

Fast by the royal standard,
　　O'erlooking all the war,
195　Lars Porsena of Clusium
　　Sat in his ivory car.
By the right wheel rode Mamilius,
　　Prince of the Latian name;

---

[1] *Umbrian.* Umbria was a division of Italy, lying to the east of Etruria. See Frontispiece.

[2] *Gaul.* About this time the Gauls were crossing the Alps from France and Germany, and settling in northern Italy. See Frontispiece.

[3] *Port and vest.* Bearing and dress.

[4] *Lucumo.* Prince or noble.

[5] *Fourfold shield.* Made of four thicknesses of ox-hide.

[6] *Brand.* Sword.

[7] *Thrasymene.* The largest lake in Etruria, about thirty miles in

And by the left false Sextus,[1]
    That wrought the deed of shame.

25

But when the face of Sextus
    Was seen among the foes,
A yell that rent the firmament
    From all the town arose.
On the house-tops was no woman
    But spat towards him and hissed,
No child but screamed out curses,
    And shook its little fist.

26

But the Consul's brow was sad,
    And the Consul's speech was low,
And darkly looked he at the wall,
    And darkly at the foe.
"Their van will be upon us
    Before the bridge goes down;
And if they once may win the bridge,
    What hope to save the town?"

28

225 "And for the tender mother
       Who dandled him to rest,
     And for the wife who nurses
       His baby at her breast,
     And for the holy maidens [1]
230   Who feed the eternal flame,
     To save them from false Sextus
       That wrought the deed of shame?

29

     "Hew down the bridge, Sir Consul,
       With all the speed ye may;
235 I, with two more to help me,
       Will hold the foe in play.
     In yon strait path a thousand
       May well be stopped by three.
     Now who will stand on either hand,
240   And keep the bridge with me?"

30

     Then out spake Spurius Lartius;
       A Ramnian [2] proud was he:

---

[1] *Holy maidens.* The Vestal Virgins or Priestesses of the goddess Vesta, whose duty it was to guard the sacred fire that was kept by them always burning on the altar of the goddess. It was believed that the extinguishing of this fire meant the ruin of Rome. The priestesses, of whom there were six, were held in special reverence, and had many privileges. They were sworn never to marry; if they did so, they paid the penalty of breaking their oath by being buried alive. Vesta was worshipped in Rome as the protectress of the home. A beautiful temple was erected in her honor in the Forum.

"Lo, I will stand at thy right hand,
  And keep the bridge with thee."
And out spake strong Herminius;
  Of Titian blood was he:
"I will abide on thy left side,
  And keep the bridge with thee."

31

"Horatius," quoth the Consul,
  "As thou sayest, so let it be."
And straight against that great array
  Forth went the dauntless Three.
For Romans in Rome's quarrel
  Spared neither land nor gold,
Nor son nor wife, nor limb nor life,
  In the brave days of old.

32

Then none was for a party;
  Then all were for the state;
Then the great man helped the poor,
  And the poor man loved the great:
Then lands [1] were fairly portioned;
  Then spoils [2] were fairly sold:

---

were divided: the *Ramnes*, or descendants of the Latins; the *Tities*, or descendants of the Sabines; and the *Luceres*, or descendants of the Etruscans. The Romans were a mixed people, made up principally of Latins, Sabines, and Etruscans.

[1] *Lands.* The public lands were principally acquired by conquest, and were supposed to be let without favor to the citizens at a certain rental. It was one of the main grievances of the common people, or *Plebeians*, against the nobles, or *Patricians*, that the latter had their undue share of these public lands.

[2] *Spoils.* Booty captured in war, which was supposed to be sold and the proceeds fairly divided among all the citizens. The reference

The Romans were like brothers
In the brave days of old.

33

265 Now Roman is to Roman
    More hateful than a foe,
    And the Tribunes [1] beard the high,
    And the Fathers grind the low.
    As we wax hot in faction,
270   In battle we wax cold:
    Wherefore men fight not as they fought
    In the brave days of old.

34

    Now while the Three were tightening
    Their harness [2] on their backs,
275 The Consul was the foremost man
    To take in hand an axe:
    And Fathers mixed with Commons
    Seized hatchet, bar, and crow,
    And smote upon the planks above,
280   And loosed the props below.

---

here is probably to the dissatisfaction of the Plebeians at the way in which Camillus had disposed of the spoils taken at the capture of Veii. He is said to have sold the spoils, and instead of dividing the proceeds among the people, to have placed the money in the public treasury. He was also accused of having taken for his own use the great bronze gates of the city. Public opinion was so strong against him that he was forced to go into exile.

[1] *Tribunes.* Magistrates elected by the Plebeians themselves,

35

    Meanwhile the Tuscan army,
        Right glorious to behold,
    Came flashing back the noonday light,
    Rank behind rank, like surges bright
285   Of a broad sea of gold.
    Four hundred trumpets sounded
        A peal of warlike glee,
    As that great host, with measured tread,
    And spears advanced, and ensigns spread,
290   Rolled slowly towards the bridge's head,
        Where stood the dauntless Three.

36

    The Three stood calm and silent,
        And looked upon the foes,
    And a great shout of laughter
295   From all the vanguard rose;
    And forth three chiefs came spurring
        Before that deep array;
    To earth they sprang, their swords they drew,
    And lifted high their shields, and flew
300   To win the narrow way;

37

    Aunus from green Tifernum,[1]
        Lord of the Hill of Vines;
    And Seius, whose eight hundred slaves
        Sicken in Ilva's mines;[2]

---

[1] *Tifernum.* An Umbrian town on the Tiber, near the borders of Etruria.

[2] *Ilva's mines.* The iron mines of the island of Ilva, or Elba, off the coast of Etruria.

305 　　And Picus, long to Clusium
　　　　　Vassal in peace and war,
　　　　Who led to fight his Umbrian powers
　　　　From that grey crag where, girt with towers,
　　　　The fortress of Nequinum [1] lowers
310 　　　　O'er the pale waves of Nar.[2]

38

　　　　Stout Lartius hurled down Aunus
　　　　　Into the stream beneath:
　　　　Herminius struck at Seius,
　　　　　And clove him to the teeth:
315 　　At Picus brave Horatius
　　　　　Darted one fiery thrust;
　　　　And the proud Umbrian's gilded arms
　　　　　Clashed in the bloody dust.

39

　　　　Then Ocnus of Falerii [3]
320 　　　Rushed on the Roman Three;
　　　　And Lausulus of Urgo,[4]
　　　　　The rover of the sea;[5]
　　　　And Aruns of Volsinium,[6]
　　　　　Who slew the great wild boar,

---

[1] *Nequinum.* A city about fifty-six miles from Rome, situated on a steep and lofty hill overlooking the river Nar.

[2] *Nar.* Now the Nera, a tributary of the Tiber.

　　"Nar white with its sulphurous waters." — Virgil.

[3] *Falerii.* One of the cities of the Etruscan League, a few miles from Mount Soracte.

[4] *Urgo.* A small island in the Mediterranean about twenty miles

40

      Herminius smote down Aruns:
330   Lartius laid Ocnus low:
      Right to the heart of Lausulus
         Horatius sent a blow.
      "Lie there," he cried, "fell pirate!
         No more, aghast and pale,
335   From Ostia's walls the crowd shall mark
      The track of thy destroying bark.
      No more Campania's hinds[3] shall fly
      To woods and caverns when they spy
         Thy thrice accursed sail."

41

340   But now no sound of laughter
         Was heard among the foes.
      A wild and wrathful clamor
         From all the vanguard rose.
      Six spears' lengths from the entrance
345   Halted that deep array,
      And for a space no man came forth
         To win the narrow way.

---

[1] *Cosa.* A seaport town of Etruria, now known as Ansedonia.

[2] *Albinia's shore.* The Albinia is one of the rivers of Etruria, flowing into the sea.

[3] *Campania's hinds.* The peasants of Campania, the district along the sea-shore south of Latium. See Frontispiece.

42

But hark! the cry is Astur:
  And lo! the ranks divide;
And the great Lord of Luna
  Comes with his stately stride.
Upon his ample shoulders
  Clangs loud the fourfold shield,
And in his hand he shakes the brand
  Which none but he can wield.

43

He smiled on those bold Romans
  A smile serene and high;
He eyed the flinching Tuscans,
  And scorn was in his eye.
Quoth he, "The she-wolf's litter [1]
  Stand savagely at bay:
But will ye dare to follow,
  If Astur clears the way?"

The Tuscans raised a joyful cry
    To see the red blood flow.

45

            He reeled, and on Herminius
375   He leaned one breathing-space;
        Then, like a wild-cat mad with wounds,
            Sprang right at Astur's face.
        Through teeth, and skull, and helmet,
            So fierce a thrust he sped,
380   The good sword stood a hand-breadth out
            Behind the Tuscan's head.

46

        And the great Lord of Luna
            Fell at that deadly stroke,
        As falls on Mount Alvernus [1]
385   A thunder-smitten oak.
        Far o'er the crashing forest
            The giant arms lie spread;
        And the pale augurs,[2] muttering low,
            Gaze on the blasted head.

47

390   On Astur's throat Horatius
            Right firmly pressed his heel,
        And thrice and four times tugged amain,
            Ere he wrenched out the steel.

---

[1] *Mount Alvernus.* A heavily wooded hill in the Apennines, near the source of the Tiber.

[2] *Augurs.* A body of priests at Rome who were entrusted with the duty of reading the future by observing any unusual occurrences, such as the flight of birds, the lightning, etc. No act of any public importance was undertaken by the Romans without finding from the augurs whether the signs were favorable.

"And see," he cried, "the welcome,
    Fair guests, that waits you here!
What noble Lucumo comes next
    To taste our Roman cheer?"

48

But at his haughty challenge
    A sullen murmur ran,
Mingled of wrath and shame and dread,
    Along that glittering van.
There lacked not men of prowess,
    Nor men of lordly race;
For all Etruria's noblest
    Were round the fatal place.

49

But all Etruria's noblest
    Felt their hearts sink to see
On the earth the bloody corpses,
    In the path the dauntless Three:
And, from the ghastly entrance
    Where those bold Romans stood,
All shrank, like boys who unaware,
Ranging the woods to start a hare,
Come to the mouth of the dark lair
Where, growling low, a fierce old bear
    Lies amidst bones and blood.

50

Was none who would be foremost
    To lead such dire attack:
But those behind cried "Forward!"
    And those before cried "Back!"
And backward now and forward
    Wavers the deep array;

And on the tossing sea of steel,
   To and fro the standards reel;
And the victorious trumpet-peal
   Dies fitfully away.

51

Yet one man for one moment
   Stood out before the crowd;
Well known was he to all the Three,
   And they gave him greeting loud,
"Now welcome, welcome, Sextus!
   Now welcome to thy home!
Why dost thou stay, and turn away?
   Here lies the road to Rome."

52

Thrice looked he at the city;
   Thrice looked he at the dead;
And thrice came on in fury,
   And thrice turned back in dread;
And, white with fear and hatred,
   Scowled at the narrow way
Where, wallowing in a pool of blood,
   The bravest Tuscans lay.

53

But meanwhile axe and lever
   Have manfully been plied;
And now the bridge hangs tottering
   Above the boiling tide.
"Come back, come back, Horatius!"
   Loud cried the Fathers all.
"Back, Lartius! back, Herminius!
   Back, ere the ruin fall!"

54

Back darted Spurius Lartius;
　Herminius darted back:
And, as they passed, beneath their feet
　They felt the timbers crack.
But when they turned their faces,
　And on the farther shore
Saw brave Horatius stand alone,
　They would have crossed once more.

55

But with a crash like thunder
　Fell every loosened beam,
And, like a dam, the mighty wreck
　Lay right athwart the stream;
And a long shout of triumph
　Rose from the walls of Rome,
As to the highest turret-tops
　Was splashed the yellow foam.

56

And, like a horse unbroken
　When first he feels the rein,
The furious river struggled hard,
　And tossed his tawny mane,
And burst the curb, and bounded,
　Rejoicing to be free,
And whirling down, in fierce career,
Battlement, and plank, and pier,
　Rushed headlong to the sea.

57

Alone stood brave Horatius,
　But constant still in mind;

Thrice thirty thousand foes before,
    And the broad flood behind.
"Down with him!" cried false Sextus,
    With a smile on his pale face.
"Now yield thee," cried Lars Porsena,
    "Now yield thee to our grace."

58

Round turned he, as not deigning
    Those craven ranks to see;
Naught spake he to Lars Porsena,
    To Sextus naught spake he;
But he saw on Palatinus [1]
    The white porch of his home;
And he spake to the noble river
    That rolls by the towers of Rome.

59

"O Tiber! father Tiber! [2]
    To whom the Romans pray,
A Roman's life, a Roman's arms,
    Take thou in charge this day!"
So he spake, and speaking sheathed
    The good sword by his side,
And with his harness on his back
    Plunged headlong in the tide.

60

No sound of joy or sorrow
    Was heard from either bank;

---

[1] *Palatinus.* One of the seven hills of Rome. See Map, page 6. At this time the dwellings of the principal Patrician families were situated on this hill.

[2] *Father Tiber.* The river was worshipped by the Romans as a god.

But friends and foes in dumb surprise,
With parted lips and straining eyes,
  Stood gazing where he sank;
And when above the surges
  They saw his crest appear,
All Rome sent forth a rapturous cry,
And even the ranks of Tuscany
  Could scarce forbear to cheer.

61

But fiercely ran the current,
  Swollen high by months of rain:
And fast his blood was flowing,
  And he was sore in pain,
And heavy with his armor,
  And spent with changing¹ blows:
And oft they thought him sinking,
  But still again he rose.

62

Never, I ween,² did swimmer,
  In such an evil case,
Struggle through such a raging flood
  Safe to the landing-place:
But his limbs were borne up bravely
  By the brave heart within,
And our good father Tiber
  Bore bravely up his chin.

But for this stay, ere close of day
   We should have sacked the town!"
"Heaven help him!" quoth Lars Porsena,
   "And bring him safe to shore;
For such a gallant feat of arms
   Was never seen before."

64

And now he feels the bottom;
   Now on dry earth he stands;
Now round him throng the Fathers
   To press his gory hands;
And now, with shouts and clapping,
   And noise of weeping loud,
He enters through the River-Gate,
   Borne by the joyous crowd.

65

They gave him of the corn-land,
   That was of public right,[1]
As much as two strong oxen[2]
   Could plough from morn till night;
And they made a molten image,
   And set it up on high,
And there it stands unto this day
   To witness if I lie.

66

Horatius in his harness,
  Halting upon one knee:
And underneath is written,
  In letters all of gold,
How valiantly he kept the bridge
  In the brave days of old.

67

And still his name sounds stirring
  Unto the men of Rome,
As the trumpet-blast that cries to them
  To charge the Volscian [1] home;
And wives still pray to Juno [2]
  For boys with hearts as bold
As his who kept the bridge so well
  In the brave days of old.

68

And in the nights of winter,
  When the cold north-winds blow,
And the long howling of the wolves
  Is heard amidst the snow;
When round the lonely cottage
  Roars loud the tempest's din,

Palatine, the Capitoline, and the Quirinal hills. It was originally a marsh, but was drained by one of the early kings, and set apart as a public meeting place. Around the open space were built shops, temples, and public buildings. See Map, page 6.

[1] *Volscian.* The Volsci were one of the ancient peoples of Italy, with whom the Romans waged war for many years. Their territory was adjacent to that of Rome. At the time this Lay was supposed to have been sung, the Romans had inflicted a severe defeat on the Volscians. See Frontispiece.

[2] *Juno.* The wife of Jupiter, the king of the gods, and one of the supreme deities of the Romans. She was worshipped as the goddess of marriage and childbirth.

And the good logs of Algidus [1]
   Roar louder yet within;

69

When the oldest cask is opened,
   And the largest lamp is lit;
When the chestnuts glow in the embers,
   And the kid turns on the spit;
When young and old in circle
   Around the firebrands close;
When the girls are weaving baskets,
   And the lads are shaping bows;

70

When the goodman mends his armor,
   And trims his helmet's plume;
When the goodwife's shuttle merrily
   Goes flashing through the loom,—
With weeping and with laughter
   Still is the story told,
How well Horatius kept the bridge
   In the brave days of old.

---

[1] *Algidus.* A part of the Alban Hills, about twelve miles from Rome.

INTRODUCTION
TO
THE BATTLE OF THE LAKE REGILLUS

AFTER the abandoning of the siege of Rome by Porsena and the Etruscan armies, Tarquin withdrew to Tusculum, where he lived for ten years with his son-in-law, Mamilius. During this time he was engaged in binding together the Latin cities in a league strong enough to assist him in another attempt to regain his throne. At last he was successful; the Latin cities agreed to join together, and to march, under the leadership of Mamilius of Tusculum, against Rome. Tarquin, now a very old man, accompanied the army, and with him were his two sons, Titus and Sextus.

The Romans, under the leadership of Aulus Postumius, with Titus Æbutius as second in command, marched to meet the Latins. The two armies faced each other at Lake Regillus, and the Romans were successful. Mamilius, Titus, and Sextus were slain, and the aged king fled from the field of battle. The Romans made peace with the Latin cities on the condition that they would no longer aid Tarquin, and would refuse him a shelter. The old king was now completely broken down; his sons were dead and his friends had deserted him. Accompanied by a few followers, he fled to Cumæ, on the Bay of Naples, where he died a year later, fourteen years after he had been banished from Rome.

Macaulay says: "The popular belief at Rome, from an early period, seems to have been that the great day of Regillus was decided by supernatural agency. Castor and Pollux, it was said, had fought, armed and mounted, at the head of the legions of the commonwealth, and had afterwards carried the news of the victory with incredible speed to the city. The well in the Forum at which they had alighted was pointed out. Near the well rose their ancient temple. A great festival was kept in their honor on the Ides of Quintilis, supposed to be the anniversary of the battle; and on that day sumptuous sacrifices were offered to them at the public charge. One spot on the margin of Lake Regillus was regarded during many ages with superstitious awe. A mark, resembling in shape a horse's hoof, was discernible in the volcanic rock; and this mark was believed to have been made by one of the celestial chargers."

LICTORS

The twin gods, Castor and Pollux, were the sons of Zeus, or Jupiter, and Leda, and were born in Sparta. They performed during life many bold and daring exploits, and after death were placed in the heavens as the constellation *Gemini* or the Twins. Divine honors were paid to them at Sparta, and in many other Greek cities, where temples were erected in their honor. They were specially worshipped as the protectors of sailors while at sea. The brothers usually appeared riding side by side on white horses, armed with spears, and on the head of each a cap, on which glittered a single star.

The anniversary of the battle of Lake Regillus was celebrated with great splendor at Rome. The knights met at the temple of Mars outside the walls, and rode in procession through the city to the temple of Castor in the Forum. Each knight, mounted on a magnificent horse, was clothed in purple and crowned with olive. Sometimes as many as five thousand knights took part in the procession. This pageant was, during several centuries, considered as one of the most splendid sights of Rome.

The Battle of the Lake Regillus is supposed to have been composed in connection with one of these great religious celebrations. "Songs," says Macaulay, "were chanted at the religious festivals of Rome from an early period. It was therefore likely that the pontiffs, when they had resolved to add a grand procession of knights to the other solemnities performed on the Ides of Quintilis, would call in the aid of a poet. Such a poet would naturally take for his subject the battle of Regillus, the appearance of the Twin Gods, and the institution of their festival."

Mr. W. J. Rolfe has the following note on the knights who took such an important part in the festival: "The knights were originally the cavalry of the state, who received a horse and a sum of money for its annual support. To serve in this cavalry one must have an independent fortune, and the horses were usually assigned to young men of senatorial families. There were but six centuries of equites in Rome up to the time of the sixth king, Servius Tullius, who added taken by foreign cavalry. In 304 B.C. a second class of equites arose, who had to furnish their own horses. They were mostly wealthy young men of non-senatorial families, and were not included in the eighteen equestrian centuries. From this last class of equites grew up in later times the *Equestrian Order*, a monied aristocracy occupying a position in the state between the nobility and the common people. The members of the equestrian order wore a narrow purple stripe on the tunic and a gold ring, and the first fourteen rows of seats in the theatre behind the orchestra were given to them. On the occasion of the solemn procession to commemorate the battle of Lake Regillus, the knights were not only crowned with olive, but wore also the insignia of their rank and deeds."

THE BATTLE OF THE LAKE REGILLUS

A LAY SUNG AT THE FEAST OF CASTOR AND POLLUX, ON THE IDES OF QUINTILIS, IN THE YEAR OF THE CITY [1] CCCCLI

1

Ho, trumpets, sound a war-note!
Ho, lictors,[2] clear the way!
The Knights[3] will ride in all their pride
Along the streets to-day.
5   To-day the doors and windows
Are hung with garlands all,
From Castor[4] in the Forum[5]
To Mars[6] without the wall.

---

[1] *Year of the city.* 302 B.C. See Note 1, page 21.

[2] *Lictors.* The personal attendants, or body-guard, of the chief Roman magistrates. Their duty was to clear the way for the magistrates, to preserve order, and to carry out judicial sentences. Each lictor, as a sign of his office, carried over his shoulder the *Fasces*, an axe enclosed in a bundle of rods tied with a red strap. See Illustration, page 50.

[3] *The Knights.* See Introduction, page 51.

[4] *Castor.* The temple of Castor and Pollux, usually known as the temple of Castor, was on the south side of the Roman Forum, while the temple of Mars was without the walls of the city. Three beautiful pillars of the temple of Castor are still standing.

[5] *Forum.* An open space in Rome between the Palatine and Capitoline hills. It was surrounded by temples and public buildings, and it was here that the business of the state was transacted. See Map, page 6.

[6] *Mars.* One of the chief divinities of the Romans, by whom, as

>   Each Knight is robed in purple,
> 10   With olive each is crowned;
>   A gallant war-horse under each
>   Paws haughtily the ground.
>   While flows the Yellow River,[1]
>   While stands the Sacred Hill,[2]
> 15 The proud Ides of Quintilis[3]
>   Shall have such honor still.
>   Gay are the Martian Kalends:[4]
>   December Nones[5] are gay:
>   But the proud Ides, when the squadron rides,
> 20   Shall be Rome's whitest day.[6]

---

[1] *Yellow River.* The Tiber. See Note 1, page 27.

[2] *Sacred Hill.* In 494 B.C. a bitter quarrel arose between the Senate and the Plebeians, which ended in the latter withdrawing from Rome, and taking up their residence on a small hill about three miles northeast of the city. It was their intention to found another city as a rival to Rome. The Senate was forced to yield to the Plebeians, who consented to return to their homes. The hill from that time was known as the *Mons Sacer*, or the "Sacred Hill."

[3] *Ides of Quintilis.* The fifteenth day of July. Quintilis (*Quintus* — five) was the fifth month of the Roman year, which began in March. The Ides divided the month into two nearly equal parts and fell on the 13th, except in the months of March, May, July, and October, when they occurred on the 15th. The battle of the Lake Regillus was fought on the Ides of Quintilis.

[4] *Martian Kalends.* The first day of March, the New Year's Day of the Romans. On this day two great religious festivals were held, the one in honor of Vesta, and the other in honor of Juno. The Kalends were the first day of each month.

[5] *December Nones.* The fifth day of December. The Nones occurred always on the ninth day before the Ides. The festival in honor of Faunus, one of the rural divinities, took place on the Nones of December.

[6] *Whitest day.* Luckiest day, one to be marked in the calendar with white chalk. Days of ill omen were marked with charcoal.

2

Unto the Great Twin Brethren [1]
    We keep this solemn feast.
Swift, swift, the Great Twin Brethren
    Came spurring from the east.
They came o'er wild Parthenius,[2]
    Tossing in waves of pine,
O'er Cirrha's dome,[3] o'er Adria's foam,[4]
    O'er purple Apennine,
From where with flutes and dances
    Their ancient mansion rings,
In lordly Lacedæmon,[5]
    The City of two kings,
To where, by Lake Regillus,[6]
    Under the Porcian height,
All in the lands of Tusculum,[7]
    Was fought the glorious fight.

3

Now on the place of slaughter
    Are cots and sheepfolds seen,

---

[1] *Great Twin Brethren.* See Introduction, page 50.

[2] *Parthenius.* A mountain range, north of Sparta in Greece.

[3] *Cirrha's dome.* Cirrha was the port of Delphi, in Greece, the seat of the famous oracle of the god Apollo. The reference is to the dome of the temple of Apollo at Delphi, which Macaulay appears to regard as one city with Cirrha.

[4] *Adria's foam.* The Adriatic Sea.

[5] *Lacedæmon.* Sparta, or Lacedæmon, in Greece, was the birthplace of Castor and Pollux. It was the chief city of southern Greece, and was ruled jointly by two kings, descendants of the famous hero, Hercules.

[6] *Lake Regillus.* The site of the battle is unknown, as the lake has long since disappeared. The author locates the lake near the Porcian height, now known as the Monte Porzio, about ten miles from Rome.

[7] *Tusculum.* See Note 3, page 26.

And rows of vines, and fields of wheat,
    And apple-orchards green;
The swine crush the big acorns
    That fall from Corne's oaks.[1]
Upon the turf by the Fair Fount[2]
    The reaper's pottage smokes.
The fisher baits his angle;[3]
    The hunter twangs his bow;
Little they think on those strong limbs
    That moulder deep below.
Little they think how sternly
    That day the trumpets pealed;
How in the slippery swamp of blood
    Warrior and war-horse reeled;
How wolves came with fierce gallop,
    And crows on eager wings,
To tear the flesh of captains,
    And peck the eyes of kings;
How thick the dead lay scattered
    Under the Porcian height;
How through the gates of Tusculum
    Raved the wild stream of flight;
And how the Lake Regillus
    Bubbled with crimson foam,
What time the Thirty Cities[4]
    Came forth to war with Rome.

---

[1] *Corne's oaks.* Corne is a hill near Tusculum, celebrated for its oak and beech trees.

[2] *Fair Fount.* Evidently a spring in this vicinity, but which cannot be identified.

[3] *Angle.* Fish-hook.

[4] *Thirty Cities.* The Latin Confederacy was composed of thirty cities, similar to the twelve cities of the Etruscan League mentioned in *Horatius.* Rome was originally at the head of the Confederacy, but after the expulsion of the Tarquins, the other cities combined

4

65 But, Roman, when thou standest
  Upon that holy ground,
 Look thou with heed on the dark rock
  That girds the dark lake round,
 So shalt thou see a hoof-mark [1]
70 Stamped deep into the flint:
 It was no hoof of mortal steed
  That made so strange a dint:
 There to the Great Twin Brethren
  Vow thou thy vows, and pray
75 That they, in tempest and in fight,
  Will keep thy head alway.

5

 Since last the Great Twin Brethren
  Of mortal eyes were seen,
 Have years gone by an hundred
80 And fourscore and thirteen.
 That summer a Virginius [2]
  Was Consul first in place; [3]
 The second was stout Aulus,
  Of the Posthumian race.
85 The Herald of the Latines
  From Gabii [4] came in state:

---

against the Romans, under the leadership of Octavius Mamilius, in the effort to restore the rule of the Tarquins in Rome.

[1] *Hoof-mark.* See Introduction, page 50.

[2] *Virginius.* A member of the Patrician family of the Virginii.

[3] *First in place.* The two Consuls had equal rights and authority, seniority being determined probably by age, or perhaps by the number of votes received in the elections.

[4] *Gabii.* One of the Latin cities, about twelve miles east of Rome.

The Herald of the Latines
 Passed through Rome's Eastern Gate:[1]
The Herald of the Latines
90   Did in our Forum stand;
And there he did his office,
 A sceptre[2] in his hand.

6

"Hear, Senators and people
 Of the good town of Rome,
95 The Thirty Cities charge you
 To bring the Tarquins home;
And if ye still be stubborn,
 To work the Tarquins wrong,
The Thirty Cities warn you,
100 Look that your walls be strong."

7

Then spake the Consul Aulus,
 He spake a bitter jest:
"Once the jay sent a message
 Unto the eagle's nest:—
105 Now yield thou up thine eyrie
 Unto the carrion-kite,
Or come forth valiantly, and face
 The jays in deadly fight.—
Forth looked in wrath the eagle;
110 And carrion-kite and jay,
Soon as they saw his beak and claw
 Fled screaming far away."

---

[1] *Eastern Gate.* The *Porta Esquilina*, through which one would enter coming from Gabii. See Map, page 6.

[2] *Sceptre.* The sign of his authority as official spokesman for the Thirty Cities.

8

      The Herald of the Latines
        Hath hied him back in state;
115   The Fathers of the City
        Are met in high debate.
      Thus spake the elder Consul,
        An ancient man and wise:
      "Now hearken, Conscript Fathers,[1]
120   To that which I advise.
      In seasons of great peril
        'Tis good that one bear sway;
      Then choose we a Dictator,[2]
        Whom all men shall obey.
125   Camerium[3] knows how deeply
        The sword of Aulus bites,
      And all our city calls him
        The man of seventy fights.
      Then let him be Dictator
130   For six months and no more,

---

[1] *Conscript Fathers.* See Note 3, page 28.

[2] *Dictator.* In times of great peril the Romans were accustomed to choose an extraordinary officer called a Dictator, who during his six months' term of office held supreme authority both within and without the city. He was elected by the Senate on the nomination of one of the Consuls, and was allowed to name his own chief lieutenant, who was known as Master of the Knights. As a sign of his authority, the Dictator was preceded by twenty-four lictors, who carried the axe as well as the bundle of rods when within the city, to show that he had power over life and death, without any one to interfere with his actions or to question his rule.

[3] *Camerium.* One of the ancient cities of Latium, the site of which is now unknown. It was captured by Tarquin during his reign, but after his expulsion from Rome was one of the first of the Latin cities to take up his cause.

And have a Master of the Knights,
   And axes twenty-four."

9

So Aulus was Dictator,
   The man of seventy fights;
He made Æbutius Elva
   His Master of the Knights.
On the third morn thereafter,
   At dawning of the day,
Did Aulus and Æbutius
   Set forth with their array.
Sempronius Atratinus
   Was left in charge at home
With boys, and with grey-headed men,
   To keep the walls of Rome.
Hard by the Lake Regillus
   Our camp was pitched at night;
Eastward a mile the Latines lay,
   Under the Porcian height.
Far over hill and valley
   Their mighty host was spread;
And with their thousand watch-fires
   The midnight sky was red.

10

Up rose the golden morning
   Over the Porcian height,
The proud Ides of Quintilis
   Marked evermore with white.
Not without secret trouble
   Our bravest saw the foes;
For girt by threescore thousand spears,
   The thirty standards rose.

From every warlike city
  That boasts the Latian name,
Foredoomed to dogs and vultures,
  That gallant army came;
165 From Setia's [1] purple vineyards,
  From Norba's [2] ancient wall,
From the white streets of Tusculum,
  The proudest town of all;
From where the Witch's Fortress [3]
170   O'erhangs the dark-blue seas;
From the still glassy lake that sleeps
  Beneath Aricia's [4] trees —
Those trees in whose dim shadow
  The ghastly priest [5] doth reign,
175 The priest who slew the slayer,
  And shall himself be slain;

---

[1] *Setia.* One of the cities of the Latin League, now known as Sessa, situated on the slope of the Volscian Mountains. It was celebrated for its grapes, from which a famous wine was made.

[2] *Norba.* Now known as Norma, one of the cities of the Latin League, situated a short distance from Setia. The ruins of its enormous walls are still seen.

[3] *Witch's Fortress.* A cape on the sea-coast, supposed to have been the abode of Circe, the witch or enchantress who was accustomed to turn men into swine by means of a magic liquor which she gave them to drink.

[4] *Aricia.* A city in the Alban Hills about sixteen miles from Rome, now known as Ariccia. It was situated near the modern lake of Nemi, a beautiful sheet of clear water lying in the crater of an extinct volcano.

From the drear banks of Ufens,[1]
 Where flights of marsh-fowl play,
And buffaloes lie wallowing
 Through the hot summer's day;
From the gigantic watch-towers,
 No work of earthly men,
Whence Cora's[2] sentinels o'erlook
 The never-ending fen;
From the Laurentian jungle,[3]
 The wild hog's reedy home;
From the green steeps whence Anio[4] leaps
 In floods of snow-white foam.

11

Aricia, Cora, Norba,
 Velitræ,[5] with the might
Of Setia and of Tusculum,
 Were marshalled on the right:

---

[1] *Ufens.* A marshy river of Latium, rising in the Volscian Hills.

[2] *Cora.* One of the Latin cities, now known as Cori, about thirty-seven miles from Rome, on the edge of the Volscian Hills. It overlooks the Pontine Marshes, "the never-ending fen." See Note 1, page 66. The ruins of its ancient walls are enormous, and are still standing. The walls of both Cora and Norba are fabled to have been built by the giants of old, who are said to have been on the earth before it was inhabited by man.

[3] *Laurentian jungle.* Laurentum was a city on the sea-coast about ten miles from the mouth of the Tiber. There was much marsh-land and forest in its immediate neighborhood.

[4] *Anio.* A river of Latium, which rises in the Apennines and flows into the Tiber near its mouth. Near Tivoli, during the course of the river, there is a series of beautiful waterfalls.

[5] *Velitræ.* A city on a spur of the Alban Hills, overlooking the Pontine Marshes.

The leader was Mamilius,[1]
　　Prince of the Latian name;
195　Upon his head a helmet
　　Of red gold shone like flame;
　　High on a gallant charger
　　Of dark-grey hue he rode;
　　Over his gilded armor
200　　A vest of purple flowed,
　　Woven in the land of sunrise [2]
　　By Syria's [3] dark-browed daughters,
　　And by the sails of Carthage [4] brought
　　Far o'er the southern waters.

12

205　Lavinium [5] and Laurentum
　　Had on the left their post,
　　With all the banners of the marsh,
　　And banners of the coast.
　　Their leader was false Sextus,
210　　That wrought the deed of shame:
　　With restless pace and haggard face
　　To his last field he came.

---

[1] *Mamilius.* See Note 3, page 26.

[2] *Land of sunrise.* The East.

[3] *Syria.* The fine purple cloth of this time came from Tyre and Sidon, in Phœnicia, on the Syrian coast.

[4] *Carthage.* The carrying trade of the world was at this time largely in the hands of the Carthaginians, or the people of Carthage, on the north coast of Africa. Carthage was a colony of Phœnicia, but soon surpassed the parent country as a commercial power.

[5] *Lavinium.* A city about three miles from the sea-coast and seventeen miles from Rome. It was founded by Æneas, the Trojan hero, and named by him in honor of his wife, Lavinia. It was regarded as the sacred city of Latium. A small village now occupies the ancient site. See Introduction to *The Prophecy of Capys*, page 117.

Man said he saw strange visions
 Which none beside might see,
215 And that strange sounds were in his ears
 Which none might hear but he.
A woman [1] fair and stately,
 But pale as are the dead,
Oft through the watches of the night
220 Sat spinning by his bed.
And as she plied the distaff,
 In a sweet voice and low,
She sang of great old houses,
 And fights fought long ago.
225 So spun she, and so sang she,
 Until the east was grey,
Then pointed to her bleeding breast,
 And shrieked, and fled away.

13

But in the centre thickest
230 Were ranged the shields of foes,
And from the centre loudest
 The cry of battle rose.
There Tibur [2] marched and Pedum [3]
 Beneath proud Tarquin's rule,
235 And Ferentinum [4] of the rock,
 And Gabii of the pool.[5]

---

[1] *A woman.* Lucretia. See Introduction to *Horatius*, page 16.

[2] *Tibur.* An ancient city on the Anio, about twenty miles from Rome, now known as Tivoli.

[3] *Pedum.* A small city of the Latin League near Tibur.

[4] *Ferentinum.* An Etruscan city about five miles from the Tiber. Like Cora and Norma, it was celebrated for its enormous walls.

[5] *The pool.* There was formerly near Gabii a small lake, but this has long since disappeared.

There rode the Volscian succors:[1]
  There, in a dark stern ring,
The Roman exiles gathered close
240   Around the ancient king.
Though white as Mount Soracte,[2]
  When winter nights are long,
His beard flowed down o'er mail and belt,
  His heart and hand were strong;
245 Under his hoary eyebrows
  Still flashed forth quenchless rage,
And, if the lance shook in his gripe,
  'Twas more with hate than age.
Close at his side was Titus
250   On an Apulian steed,[3]
Titus, the youngest Tarquin,
  Too good for such a breed.

14

Now on each side the leaders
  Gave signal for the charge;
255 And on each side the footmen
  Strode on with lance and targe;[4]
And on each side the horsemen
  Struck their spurs deep in gore,
And front to front the armies
260   Met with a mighty roar:

  And under that great battle
   The earth with blood was red;
  And, like the Pomptine fog¹ at morn,
   The dust hung overhead;
265 And louder still and louder
   Rose from the darkened field
  The braying of the war-horns,
   The clang of sword and shield,
  The rush of squadrons sweeping
270 Like whirlwinds o'er the plain,
  The shouting of the slayers,
   And screeching of the slain.

15

  False Sextus rode out foremost;
   His look was high and bold;
275 His corselet was of bison's hide,
   Plated with steel and gold.
  As glares the famished eagle
   From the Digentian rock²
  On a choice lamb that bounds alone
280 Before Bandusia's³ flock,
  Herminius⁴ glared on Sextus,
   And came with eagle speed,

---

¹ *Pomptine fog.* The Pomptine or Pontine Marshes extended along the Volscian Mountains in the southern part of Latium. The marsh was about thirty miles long and seven miles wide. See Frontispiece.

² *Digentian rock.* A rocky hill near the junction of the Digentia with the Anio River.

Herminius on black Auster,[1]
  Brave champion on brave steed;
285 In his right hand the broadsword
  That kept the bridge so well,
And on his helm the crown he won
  When proud Fidenæ[2] fell.
Woe to the maid whose lover
290   Shall cross his path to-day!
False Sextus saw, and trembled,
  And turned, and fled away.
As turns, as flies, the woodman
  In the Calabrian brake,[3]
295 When through the reeds gleams the round eye
  Of that fell speckled snake;[4]
So turned, so fled, false Sextus,
  And hid him in the rear,
Behind the dark Lavinian ranks,
300   Bristling with crest and spear.

16

But far to north Æbutius,
  The Master of the Knights,
Gave Tubero of Norba
  To feed the Porcian kites.
305 Next under those red horse-hoofs
  Flaccus of Setia lay;

---

[1] *Auster.* The name of the South Wind among the Romans was Auster.

[2] *Fidenæ.* A city on the Tiber about five miles from Rome. It was constantly at war with Rome, but was finally subdued.

[3] *Calabrian brake.* Calabria occupied the peninsula at the southeast corner of Italy. Many venomous snakes were found in the thickly wooded country. *Brake* means thicket.

Better had he been pruning
   Among his elms [1] that day.
Mamilius saw the slaughter,
   And tossed his golden crest,
And towards the Master of the Knights
   Through the thick battle pressed.
Æbutius smote Mamilius
   So fiercely on the shield
That the great lord of Tusculum
   Well-nigh rolled on the field.
Mamilius smote Æbutius,
   With a good aim and true,
Just where the neck and shoulder join,
   And pierced him through and through;
And brave Æbutius Elva
   Fell swooning to the ground,
But a thick wall of bucklers
   Encompassed him around.
His clients [2] from the battle
   Bare him some little space,
And filled a helm from the dark lake,
   And bathed his brow and face;
And when at last he opened
   His swimming eyes to light,
Men say, the earliest word he spake
   Was, "Friends, how goes the fight?"

---

[1] *Among his elms.* Pruning the grape-vines trained to the elm trees. See Note 1, page 61.

17

But meanwhile in the centre
  Great deeds of arms were wrought;
335 There Aulus the Dictator
  And there Valerius [1] fought.
Aulus with his good broadsword
  A bloody passage cleared
To where, amidst the thickest foes,
340   He saw the long white beard.
Flat lighted that good broadsword
  Upon proud Tarquin's head.
He dropped the lance; he dropped the reins;
  He fell as fall the dead.
345 Down Aulus springs to slay him,
  With eyes like coals of fire;
But faster Titus hath sprung down,
  And hath bestrode his sire.
Latian captains, Roman knights,
350   Fast down to earth they spring,
And hand to hand they fight on foot
  Around the ancient king.
First Titus gave tall Cæso
  A death wound in the face;
355 Tall Cæso was the bravest man
  Of the brave Fabian race: [2]

---

[1] *Valerius.* It is generally accepted that the Valerius here mentioned is Publius Valerius, known as *Peplicola*, or the "Friend of the People." The early accounts of the history of Rome, however, state that Publius died some time before the battle of Lake Regillus. His brother Marcus was alive at this time and took part in the battle. See Introduction to *Horatius,* page 17.

Aulus slew Rex of Gabii,
    The priest of Juno's shrine:[1]
Valerius smote down Julius,
    Of Rome's great Julian line;[2]
Julius, who left his mansion
    High on the Velian hill,[3]
And through all turns of weal and woe
    Followed proud Tarquin still.
Now right across proud Tarquin
    A corpse was Julius laid;
And Titus groaned with rage and grief,
    And at Valerius made.
Valerius struck at Titus,
    And lopped off half his crest;
But Titus stabbed Valerius
    A span deep in the breast.
Like a mast snapped by the tempest,
    Valerius reeled and fell.
Ah! woe is me for the good house
    That loves the people well!
Then shouted loud the Latines,
    And with one rush they bore
The struggling Romans backward
    Three lances' length and more;
And up they took proud Tarquin,
    And laid him on a shield,
And four strong yeomen bare him,
    Still senseless, from the field.

---

[1] *Juno's shrine.* There was a famous temple sacred to Juno at Gabii. See Note 2, page 47.

[2] *Julian line.* Another of the great Patrician families. It is said that Iulus, or Ascanius, the son of Æneas and Venus, was the founder of the line.

[3] *Velian hill.* A spur of the Palatine Hill, on the east side of the Forum.

18

385 But fiercer grew the fighting
   Around Valerius dead;
 For Titus dragged him by the foot,
   And Aulus by the head.
 "On, Latines, on!" quoth Titus,
390 "See how the rebels fly!"
 "Romans, stand firm!" quoth Aulus,
   "And win this fight or die!
 They must not give Valerius
   To raven and to kite;
395 For aye Valerius loathed the wrong,
   And aye upheld the right;
 And for your wives and babies
   In the front rank he fell.
 Now play the men for the good house
400   That loves the people well!"

19

 Then tenfold round the body
   The roar of battle rose,
 Like the roar of a burning forest
   When a strong north-wind blows.
405 Now backward, and now forward,
   Rocked furiously the fray,
 Till none could see Valerius,
   And none wist where he lay.
 For shivered arms and ensigns
410   Were heaped there in a mound,
 And corpses stiff, and dying men
   That writhed and gnawed the ground;
 And wounded horses kicking,
   And snorting purple foam;

415 Right well did such a couch befit
A Consular [1] of Rome.

20

But north looked the Dictator;
North looked he long and hard;
And spake to Caius Cossus,[2]
420 The Captain of his Guard:
"Caius, of all the Romans
Thou hast the keenest sight;
Say, what through yonder storm of dust
Comes from the Latian right?"

21

425 Then answered Caius Cossus:
"I see an evil sight:
The banner of proud Tusculum
Comes from the Latian right;
I see the plumed horsemen;
430 And far before the rest
I see the dark-grey charger,
I see the purple vest;
I see the golden helmet
That shines far off like flame;
435 So ever rides Mamilius,
Prince of the Latian name."

22

Haste to our southward battle,
  And never draw thy rein
Until thou find Herminius,
  And bid him come amain."

23

445 So Aulus spake, and turned him
      Again to that fierce strife,
    And Caius Cossus mounted,
      And rode for death and life
    Loud clanged beneath his horse-hoofs
450   The helmets of the dead,
    And many a curdling pool of blood
      Splashed him from heel to head.
    So came he far to southward,
      Where fought the Roman host,
455 Against the banners of the marsh
      And banners of the coast.
    Like corn before the sickle
      The stout Lavinians fell,
    Beneath the edge of the true sword
460   That kept the bridge so well.

24

    "Herminius! Aulus greets thee;
      He bids thee come with speed,
    To help our central battle;
      For sore is there our need.
465 There wars the youngest Tarquin,
      And there the Crest of Flame,
    The Tusculan Mamilius,
      Prince of the Latian name.
    Valerius hath fallen fighting
470   In front of our array,

And Aulus of the seventy fields
   Alone upholds the day."

25

Herminius beat his bosom,
   But never a word he spake.
He clapped his hand on Auster's mane,
   He gave the reins a shake,
Away, away went Auster,
   Like an arrow from the bow;
Black Auster was the fleetest steed
   From Aufidus to Po.[1]

26

Right glad were all the Romans
   Who, in that hour of dread,
Against great odds bare up the war
   Around Valerius dead,
When from the south the cheering
   Rose with a mighty swell:
"Herminius comes, Herminius,
   Who kept the bridge so well!"

27

Mamilius spied Herminius,
   And dashed across the way.
"Herminius! I have sought thee
   Through many a bloody day.
One of us two, Herminius,
   Shall never more go home.

---

[1] *From Aufidus to Po.* In all Italy. Aufidus was a river in the southern part of Italy, and the Po flows through the northern part of the country.

495   I will lay on for Tusculum,
      And lay thou on for Rome!"

28

    All round them paused the battle,
      While met in mortal fray
    The Roman and the Tusculan,
500   The horses black and grey.
    Herminius smote Mamilius
      Through breast-plate and through breast;
    And fast flowed out the purple blood
      Over the purple vest.
505 Mamilius smote Herminius
      Through head-piece and through head;
    And side by side those chiefs of pride
      Together fell down dead.
    Down fell they dead together
510   In a great lake of gore;
    And still stood all who saw them fall
      While men might count a score.

29

    Fast, fast, with heels wild spurning,
      The dark-grey charger fled;
515 He burst through ranks of fighting men,
      He sprang o'er heaps of dead.
    His bridle far out-streaming,
      His flanks all blood and foam,
    He sought the southern mountains,[1]
520   The mountains of his home.
    The pass was steep and rugged,
      The wolves they howled and whined;

---

[1] *Southern mountains.* The Alban Mountains, a series of volcanic hills to the south-east of Rome.

But he ran like a whirlwind up the pass,
  And he left the wolves behind.
Through many a startled hamlet
  Thundered his flying feet;
He rushed through the gate of Tusculum,
  He rushed up the long white street;
He rushed by tower and temple,
  And paused not from his race
Till he stood before his master's door
  In the stately market-place.
And straightway round him gathered
  A pale and trembling crowd,
And when they knew him, cries of rage
  Brake forth, and wailing loud:
And women rent their tresses
  For their great prince's fall;
And old men girt on their old swords,
  And went to man the wall.

30

But, like a graven image,
  Black Auster kept his place,
And ever wistfully he looked
  Into his master's face.
The raven mane that daily,
  With pats and fond caresses,
The young Herminia washed and combed,
  And twined in even tresses,
And decked with colored ribands
  From her own gay attire,
Hung sadly o'er her father's corpse
  In carnage and in mire.
Forth with a shout sprang Titus,
  And seized black Auster's rein.

555 Then Aulus sware a fearful oath,
    And ran at him amain.
    "The furies[1] of thy brother
    With me and mine abide,
    If one of your accursed house
560   Upon black Auster ride!"
    As on an Alpine watch-tower
    From heaven comes down the flame,
    Full on the neck of Titus
    The blade of Aulus came;
565 And out the red blood spouted,
    In a wide arch and tall,
    As spouts a fountain in the court
    Of some rich Capuan's hall.[2]
    The knees of all the Latines
570   Were loosened with dismay
    When dead, on dead Herminius,
    The bravest Tarquin lay.

31

    And Aulus the Dictator
    Stroked Auster's raven mane,
575 With heed he looked unto the girths,
    With heed unto the rein.
    "Now bear me well, black Auster,
    Into yon thick array;

---

[1] *The furies.* The Eumenides or Furies were the instruments of the gods for the punishment of crime. They were represented as having serpents instead of hair. In one hand they carried a torch, and in the other a whip of scorpions. Sextus is supposed to be given over to the furies as a punishment for his crime.

[2] *Capuan's hall.* Capua was an extremely wealthy and luxurious city, the capital of Campania, the district on the sea-coast to the south of Latium. See Frontispiece.

And thou and I will have revenge
    For thy good lord this day."

32

So spake he; and was buckling
    Tighter black Auster's band,
When he was aware of a princely pair
    That rode at his right hand.
So like they were, no mortal
    Might one from other know;
White as snow their armor was,
    Their steeds were white as snow.
Never on earthly anvil
    Did such rare armor gleam;
And never did such gallant steeds
    Drink of an earthly stream.

33

And all who saw them trembled,
    And pale grew every cheek;
And Aulus the Dictator
    Scarce gathered voice to speak.
"Say by what name men call you?
    What city is your home?
And wherefore ride ye in such guise
    Before the ranks of Rome?"

34

605   Our house in gay Tarentum [1]
      Is hung each morn with flowers;
    High o'er the masts of Syracuse [2]
      Our marble portal towers;
    But by the proud Eurotas [3]
610   Is our dear native home;
    And for the right we come to fight
      Before the ranks of Rome."

35

    So answered those strange horsemen,
      And each couched low his spear;
615   And forthwith all the ranks of Rome
      Were bold, and of good cheer.
    And on the thirty armies
      Came wonder and affright,
    And Ardea [4] wavered on the left,
620   A Cordan on the right.
    "Rome to the charge!" cried Aulus;
      "The foe begins to yield!
    Charge for the hearth of Vesta! [5]
    Charge for the Golden Shield! [6]

---

[1] *Tarentum.* A Greek city in Calabria, noted for its excellent harbor and its commerce. See Map, page 114.

[2] *Syracuse.* An important and wealthy city on the east coast of Sicily, celebrated for its harbor. See Map, page 114.

[3] *Eurotas.* A river of Laconia, in Greece, on the banks of which was situated Lacedæmon, or Sparta. See Note 5, page 55. The places mentioned in this section are all Greek cities, originally founded by the Dorians, and so given to the worship of Castor and Pollux. See Introduction, page 42.

[4] *Ardea.* A city near the sea-coast, about twenty-four miles from Rome. It was while Tarquin was engaged in besieging this city that he lost his throne. See Introduction to *Horatius*, page 15.

[5] *Hearth of Vesta.* See Note 1, page 33.

[6] *Golden Shield.* See Note 4, page 25.

625   Let no man stop to plunder,
        But slay, and slay, and slay;
      The gods who live forever
        Are on our side to-day."

36

      Then the fierce trumpet-flourish
630   From earth to heaven arose.
      The kites know well the long stern swell
        That bids the Roman close.
      Then the good sword of Aulus
        Was lifted up to slay;
635   Then, like a crag down Apennine,
        Rushed Auster through the fray.
      But under those strange horsemen
        Still thicker lay the slain;
      And after those strange horses
640   Black Auster toiled in vain.
      Behind them Rome's long battle
        Came rolling on the foe,
      Ensigns dancing wild above,
        Blades all in line below.
645   So comes the Po in flood-time
        Upon the Celtic plain;[1]
      So comes the squall, blacker than night,
        Upon the Adrian main.
      Now, by our Sire Quirinus,[2]
650   It was a goodly sight

---

[1] *Celtic plain.* The plain of Cisalpine Gaul, one of the divisions of northern Italy through which the Po flows. See Frontispiece.

[2] *Sire Quirinus.* Romulus, the founder of Rome, was carried away to heaven by his father, the god Mars, during a thunder-storm. Soon afterwards he appeared in a vision to a Roman Senator, and gave instructions that divine honors should be paid to him under the name

To see the thirty standards
  Swept down the tide of flight.
So flies the spray of Adria
  When the black squall doth blow,
655 So corn-sheaves in the flood-time
  Spin down the whirling Po.
False Sextus to the mountains
  Turned first his horse's head;
And fast fled Ferentinum,
660   And fast Lanuvium fled.
The horsemen of Nomentum [1]
  Spurred hard out of the fray;
The footmen of Velitræ
  Threw shield and spear away.
665 And underfoot was trampled,
  Amidst the mud and gore,
The banner of proud Tusculum,
  That never stooped before.
And down went Flavius Faustus,
670   Who led his stately ranks
From where the apple-blossoms wave
  On Anio's echoing banks,
And Tullus of Arpinum,[2]
  Chief of the Volscian aids,
675 And Metius with the long fair curls,
  The love of Anxur's [3] maids,
And the white head of Vulso,
  The great Arician seer,

Quirinus. He is called *Sire*, as the father or founder of Rome. See Introduction to *The Prophecy of Capys*, page 118.

[1] *Nomentum.* A city near the Tiber, about fourteen miles from Rome.

[2] *Arpinum.* A Volscian city, about forty-five miles from Rome.

[3] *Anxur.* A Volscian city on the sea-coast south of the Pontine Marshes.

      And Nepos of Laurentum,
680   The hunter of the deer;
      And in the back false Sextus
        Felt the good Roman steel,
      And wriggling in the dust he died,
        Like a worm beneath the wheel.
685   And fliers and pursuers
        Were mingled in a mass,
      And far away the battle
        Went roaring through the pass.

37

      Sempronius Atratinus
690   Sate in the Eastern Gate,
      Beside him were three Fathers,
        Each in his chair of state;[1]
      Fabius, whose nine stout grandsons
        That day were in the field,
695   And Manlius, eldest of the Twelve[2]
        Who kept the Golden Shield;
      And Sergius, the High Pontiff,[3]
        For wisdom far renowned;
      In all Etruria's colleges[4]
700   Was no such Pontiff found.

---

[1] *Chair of state.* The curule chair, or chair of state, was a chair of peculiar design used by the higher magistrates at Rome. It was originally a symbol of the kingly power, but after the expulsion of the Tarquins it was permitted to all the chief officers of the republic.

[2] *The Twelve.* The Salii. See Note 4, page 25.

[3] *High Pontiff.* The *Pontifex Maximus*, or Chief of the College of Priests among the Romans. The College was at this time composed of five priests, who had supreme control over all matters in the state affecting the worship of the gods.

[4] *Etruria's colleges.* Bodies of priests among the Etruscans. See *Horatius*, lines 66–78.

And all around the portal,
   And high above the wall,
Stood a great throng of people,
   But sad and silent all;
705   Young lads, and stooping elders
   That might not bear the mail,
Matrons with lips that quivered,
   And maids with faces pale.
Since the first gleam of daylight,
710   Sempronius had not ceased
To listen for the rushing
   Of horse-hoofs from the east.
The mist of eve was rising,
   The sun was hastening down,
715   When he was aware of a princely pair
   Fast pricking towards the town.
So like they were, man never
   Saw twins so like before;
Red with gore their armor was,
720   Their steeds were red with gore.

38

"Hail to the great Asylum![1]
   Hail to the hill-tops seven![2]
Hail to the fire that burns for aye,
   And the shield that fell from heaven!
725   This day, by Lake Regillus,
   Under the Porcian height,

---

[1] *Asylum.* After Romulus had founded Rome, he found great difficulty in peopling his new city. He accordingly opened a place of refuge on the Capitoline Hill for those who were fugitives from their own city, and so succeeded in attracting a large population.

[2] *Hill-tops seven.* The seven hills on which Rome was built. See Map, page 6.

All in the lands of Tusculum
  Was fought a glorious fight;
To-morrow your Dictator
  Shall bring in triumph home
The spoils of thirty cities
  To deck the shrines of Rome!"

39

Then burst from that great concourse
  A shout that shook the towers,
And some ran north, and some ran south,
  Crying, "The day is ours!"
But on rode these strange horsemen,
  With slow and lordly pace;
And none who saw their bearing
  Durst ask their name or race.
On rode they to the Forum,
  While laurel-boughs and flowers,
From house-tops and from windows,
  Fell on their crests in showers.
When they drew nigh to Vesta,[1]
  They vaulted down amain,
And washed their horses in the well[2]
  That springs by Vesta's fane.
And straight again they mounted,
  And rode to Vesta's door;
Then, like a blast, away they passed,
  And no man saw them more.

40

And all the people trembled,
  And pale grew every cheek;

---

[1] *Vesta.* The temple of Vesta.

[2] *The well.* A pool or well lying between the temples of Vesta and Castor.

755 And Sergius the High Pontiff
　　　Alone found voice to speak:
　　"The gods who live forever
　　　Have fought for Rome to-day!
　　These be the Great Twin Brethren
760　　To whom the Dorians[1] pray.
　　Back comes the Chief in triumph
　　　Who, in the hour of fight,
　　Hath seen the Great Twin Brethren
　　　In harness on his right.
765　Safe comes the ship[2] to haven,
　　　Through billows and through gales,
　　If once the Great Twin Brethren
　　　Sit shining on the sails.
　　Wherefore they washed their horses
770　　In Vesta's holy well,
　　Wherefore they rode to Vesta's door,
　　　I know, but may not tell.
　　Here, hard by Vesta's Temple,
　　　Build we a stately dome
775　Unto the Great Twin Brethren
　　　Who fought so well for Rome.
　　And when the months returning
　　　Bring back this day of fight,

---

[1] *The Dorians.* The people of Lacedæmon, or Sparta. The Dorians were the ancestors of the Spartans, and originally inhabited a small district in central Greece. In very early times, however, they spread over the greater part of southern Greece, and also planted many colonies abroad.

[2] *Safe comes the ship.* Castor and Pollux were worshipped as the protectors of sailors. The appearance of the light, known as *St. Elmo's Fire*, often seen on the masts and in the rigging of ships during a thunder-storm, was supposed to indicate the presence of the two gods and to be a favorable sign.

(ANSI and ISO TEST CHART No. 2)

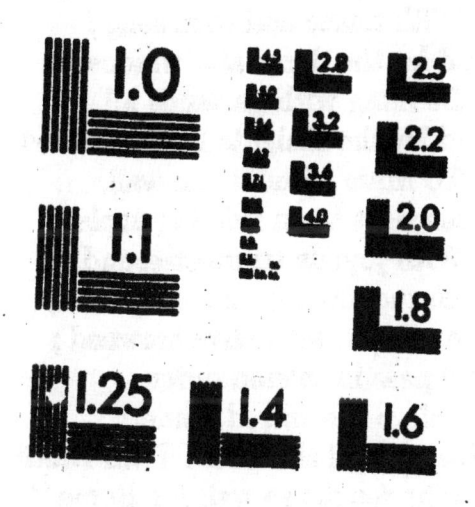

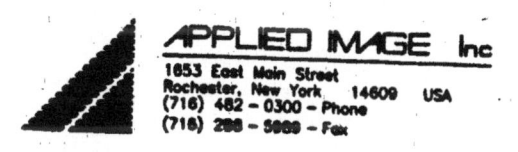

APPLIED IMAGE Inc
1653 East Main Street
Rochester, New York 14609 USA
(716) 482 - 0300 - Phone
(716) 288 - 5989 - Fax

The proud Ides of Quintilis,
780   Marked evermore with white,
Unto the Great Twin Brethren
    Let all the people throng,
With chaplets and with offerings,
    With music and with song;
785 And let the doors and windows
    Be hung with garlands all,
And let the Knights be summoned
    To Mars without the wall.
Thence let them ride in purple
790   With joyous trumpet-sound,
Each mounted on his war-horse,
    And each with olive crowned;
And pass in solemn order
    Before the sacred dome,
795 Where dwell the Great Twin Brethren
    Who fought so well for Rome!"

INTRODUCTION
TO
VIRGINIA

Lord Macaulay, in his introduction to this lay, gives an account of the historic incidents connected therewith. The story is somewhat as follows:

The population of Rome was, from a very early period, divided into hereditary castes, which indeed readily united to repel foreign enemies, but which regarded each other during many years with bitter hatred. Among the grievances under which the Plebeians suffered, three were felt as particularly severe. They were excluded from the higher magistracies, they were deprived of their share in the public lands, and they were ground in the dust by the laws dealing with debtors. The ruling class at Rome was a monied class; and it made and administered the laws with a view solely to its own interests. The great men held a large portion of the people in dependence by means of lending money at enormous interest. The law of debt in Rome was the most horrible that has ever been known among men. The liberty and even the life of the debtor who could not pay were at the mercy of the Patrician moneylenders. Children often became slaves in consequence of the misfortunes of their parents. The debtor was imprisoned, not in a public jail, but in a private workhouse, belonging to the creditor. It is said that tight that brave soldiers, whose breasts were covered with honorable scars, were often marked still more deeply on the back, by the scourges of Patrician money-lenders.

The Plebeians were, however, not wholly without legal rights. From an early period they had been admitted to some share in political power, and were allowed a small part in the election to offices from which they themselves were excluded. They also had acquired the right to elect Tribunes, who had no active share in the government, but whose power soon became formidable. The persons of the Tribunes were sacred, and they had the right to obstruct all legislation.

For more than a century after the Plebeians gained the right to elect Tribunes, they struggled manfully for the removal of their grievances, and forced concession after concession from the Patricians. At length, in 375 B.C., both parties gathered their whole strength for the last and most desperate conflict. In that year the Tribune, Caius Licinius, proposed the three laws which are called by his name, and which were intended to redress the three great grievances of the Plebeians. In his efforts he was strongly supported by his fellow Tribune, Lucius Sextius. Year after year Licinius and Sextius were reëlected Tribunes, and year after year they continued to stop the whole machinery of government. None of the chief magistrates could be elected; no military muster could be held. The Patricians did their utmost, by bribes and threats, to break up the union of the Plebeians, but the common people stood firmly together in support of their Tribunes. At length the Patricians were compelled to give way, and the Licinian Laws were passed. Lucius Sextius was the first Plebeian Consul, Caius Licinius the third.

It is but natural to suppose that, during the conflict that raged over the Licinian Laws, the poets of the people were not idle. It is probable that they employed themselves in turning into verse the speeches of the Tribunes, and in heaping abuse upon the leaders of the Patricians. One of the most violent supporters of the aristocracy in the struggle was Appius Claudius Crassus, the descendant of a noble house, which had distinguished itself in the government of the city, but which had won no military renown. In addition the grandfather of Appius Claudius had left a name as much detested among the people as that of Sextus Tarquin. It is to be understood that *Virginia* is a poem recited at this period by one of the Plebeian poets to inflame the populace against Appius Claudius, by relating a disgraceful incident in connection with the life of his grandfather, a cruel oppressor of the people.

About seventy years before this time, in order that the laws of the republic might be gathered together and written down, so that all, but especially the Plebeians, might become familiar with them, both parties agreed to give up their elective officers for a time, and to place the government in the hands of ten men known as Decemvirs (*decem*, ten). The First Decemvirate collected the laws and had them inscribed on ten tables of brass. The Second Decemvirate added two more tables, but when they had completed their work, they refused to resign and threatened to set up an absolute government in the interest of the Patrician class. The people were helpless, but an act of outrageous tyranny on the part of Appius Claudius, the leader of the Decemvirs, roused them to the utmost fury. The incident is related in the text. The Plebeians, as the easiest way out of the difficulty, removed from the city in a body, resolved to ruin the state rather than submit to the insolent tyranny of the Decemvirs. There was nothing for the Decemvirs but to resign. This they did, and the old government was restored, Consuls favorable to the Plebeians being elected.

"In order that the reader may judge fairly of these fragments of the lay of *Virginia*," says Macaulay, "he must imagine himself a Plebeian who has just voted for the election of Sextius and Licinius. All the power of the Patricians has been exerted to throw out the two great champions of the Commons. Lucius and Sextius have a fifth time carried all the tribes; work is suspended; the booths are closed; the Plebeians bear on their shoulders the two champions of liberty through the Forum. Just at this moment it is announced that a popular poet has made a new song that will cut the Claudian nobles to the heart. The crowd gathers round him, and calls on him to recite it. He takes his stand on the spot, where, according to tradition, Virginia, more than seventy years ago, was seized by the pander of Appius, and begins his story."

VIRGINIA

FRAGMENTS OF A LAY SUNG IN THE FORUM ON THE DAY WHEREON LUCIUS SEXTIUS SEXTINUS LATERANUS AND CAIUS LICINIUS CALVUS STOLO WERE ELECTED TRIBUNES OF THE COMMONS THE FIFTH TIME, IN THE YEAR OF THE CITY [1] CCCLXXXII

> YE good men of the Commons, with loving hearts and true,
> Who stand by the bold Tribunes [2] that still have stood by you,
> Come, make a circle round me, and mark my tale with care,
> A tale of what Rome once hath borne, of what Rome yet may bear.
> 5 This is no Grecian fable, of fountains running wine, [3]
> Of maids with snaky tresses, [4] or sailors turned to swine. [5]

---

[1] *Year of the city.* 371 B.C. See Note 1, page 21.

[2] *Bold Tribunes.* Lucius Sextius and Caius Licinius. See Introduction, page 88.

[3] *Fountains running wine.* "When the worship of Bacchus, the god of Wine, was introduced into Greece, it was said that his followers caused springs of wine to gush forth by striking the ground with their wands." — FLATHER.

[4] *Snaky tresses.* Both the *Furies* and the *Gorgons* among the Greeks were supposed to have snakes on their heads instead of hair. See Note 1, page 77. The Gorgons were three frightful monsters, only one of whom, Medusa, was mortal. She was slain by the Greek hero, Perseus. The story is told in Kingsley's *The Heroes.*

[5] *Turned to swine.* Circe, the Greek enchantress, so treated the

Here, in this very Forum, under the noonday sun,
In sight of all the people, the bloody deed was done.
Old men still creep among us who saw that fearful day,
10 Just seventy years and seven ago, when the wicked Ten [1] bare sway.

Of all the wicked Ten still the names are held accursed,
And of all the wicked Ten Appius Claudius was the worst.
He stalked along the Forum like King Tarquin in his pride;
Twelve axes [2] waited on him, six marching on a side;
15 The townsmen shrank to right and left, and eyed askance with fear
His lowering brow, his curling mouth, which always seemed to sneer:
That brow of hate, that mouth of scorn, marks all the kindred still;
For never was there Claudius yet but wished the Commons ill;
Nor lacks he fit attendance; for close behind his heels,
20 With outstretched chin and crouching pace, the client Marcus steals,
His loins girt up to run with speed, be the errand what it may,

---

sailors of Odysseus, the Greek hero, on his return from the Trojan war. See Note 3, page 61.

[1] *The wicked Ten.* The Decemvirs. See Introduction, page 89.

[2] *Twelve axes.* Twelve lictors. See Note 2, page 53.

And the smile flickering on his cheek, for aught his
    lord may say.
Such varlets pimp and jest for hire among the lying
    Greeks:
Such varlets still are paid to hoot when brave Li-
    cinius [1] speaks.
25 Where'er ye shed the honey, the buzzing flies will
    crowd;
Where'er ye fling the carrion, the raven's croak
    is loud;
Where'er down Tiber garbage floats, the greedy
    pike ye see;
And wheresoe'er such lord is found, such client
    still will be.

Just then, as through one cloudless chink in a
    black stormy sky,
30 Shines out the dewy morning-star, a fair young
    girl came by.
With her small tablets [2] in her hand, and her satchel
    on her arm,
Home she went bounding from the school, nor
    dreamed of shame or harm;
And past those dreaded axes she innocently ran,
With bright, frank brow that had not learned to
    blush at gaze of man;
35 And up the Sacred Street [3] she turned, and, as she
    danced along,

---

[1] *Licinius.* See Introduction, page 88.

[2] *Tablets.* Two or three small pieces of wood coated over with wax, and fastened together at the back by wires, somewhat like a book. Impressions were made on the wax with an iron pencil sharpened at one end, called a *stylus.* The other end of the pencil was broad and flat for the purpose of erasing the marks made.

[3] *Sacred Street.* To overcome the difficulty of lack of population after the founding of Rome, Romulus made of the city a refuge for

She warbled gayly to herself lines of the good old
    song,[1]
How for a sport the princes came spurring from
    the camp,
And found Lucrece, combing the fleece, under the
    midnight lamp.
The maiden sang as sings the lark, when up he
    darts his flight,
40 From his nest in the green April corn, to meet the
    morning light;
And Appius heard her sweet young voice, and saw
    her sweet young face,
And loved her with the accursed love of his ac-
    cursed race,
And all along the Forum, and up the Sacred Street,
His vulture eye pursued the trip of those small
    glancing feet.

. . . .

---

those who were compelled to leave their own homes. The population grew rapidly, but consisted principally of men. In order to obtain wives for the citizens, Romulus invited the neighboring tribes to attend a great festival to be held at Rome in honor of Jupiter. Numbers of men and women came in answer to the invitation, and especially a great many from among the Sabines. At a given signal the men of Rome rushed upon their unsuspecting guests and bore the women away in triumph to the city. The enraged Sabines waged war on Rome to recover the captives. After the war had lasted for three years, the Sabine women, who, in the meantime, had married their captors, made peace between their tribe and their husbands. The Sabines agreed to join with the Romans under the joint rule of Romulus and their own king Tatius. To commemorate the union of the two peoples, the street where the peace was signed was ever afterwards known as the *Sacred Street*. It was the most ancient and most important street in Rome.

[1] *Good old song.* See Introduction to *Horatius*, page 16.

45   Over the Alban mountains[1] the light of morning broke;
From all the roofs of the Seven Hills curled the thin wreaths of smoke.
The city-gates were opened; the Forum all alive,
With buyers and with sellers was humming like a hive.
Blithely on brass and timber the craftsman's stroke was ringing.
50 And blithely o'er her panniers the market-girl was singing,
And blithely young Virginia came smiling from her home:
Ah! woe for young Virginia, the sweetest maid in Rome!
With her small tablets in her hand, and her satchel on her arm,
Forth she went bounding to the school, nor dreamed of shame or harm.
55 She crossed the Forum shining with stalls in alleys gay,
And just had reached the very spot whereon I stand this day,
When up the varlet Marcus came; not such as when erewhile
He crouched behind his patron's heels with the true client smile:
He came with lowering forehead, swollen features, and clenched fist,
60 And strode across Virginia's path, and caught her by the wrist.
Hard strove the frighted maiden, and screamed with look aghast;

And at her scream from right and left the folk
  came running fast;
The money-changer Crispus, with his thin silver
  hairs,
And Hanno from the stately booth glittering with
  Punic wares,[1]
65 And the strong smith Muræna, grasping a half-
  forged brand,
And Volero the flesher,[2] his cleaver in his hand.
All came in wrath and wonder; for all knew that
  fair child;
And, as she passed them twice a day, all kissed
  their hands and smiled;
And the strong smith Muræna gave Marcus such a
  blow,
70 The caitiff reeled three paces back, and let the
  maiden go.
Yet glared he fiercely round him, and growled in
  harsh, fell tone,
"She's mine, and I will have her: I seek but for
  mine own:
She is my slave, born in my house, and stolen away
  and sold,
The year of the sore sickness,[3] ere she was twelve
  hours old.
75 'Twas in the sad September, the month of wail
  and fright,
Two augurs[4] were borne forth that morn; the Consul died ere night.

---

[1] *Punic wares.* Wares from Carthage. See Note 4, page 63.

[2] *Flesher.* Butcher.

[3] *Sore sickness.* During the year 463 B.C. a plague raged in Rome. This would indicate that at this time Virginia was fourteen years of age.

[4] *Augurs.* See Note 2, page 40.

VIRGINIA

I wait on Appius Claudius, I waited on his sire;
Let him who works the client wrong beware the
   patron's ire!"

   So spake the varlet Marcus; and dread and
      silence came
80 On all the people at the sound of the great Clau-
      dian name.
   For then there was no Tribune to speak the word
      of might,
   Which makes the rich man tremble, and guards
      the poor man's right.
   There was no brave Licinius, no honest Sextius
      then;
   But all the city, in great fear, obeyed the wicked
      Ten.
85 Yet ere the varlet Marcus again might seize the
      maid,
   Who clung tight to Muræna's skirt, and sobbed and
      shrieked for aid,
   Forth through the throng of gazers the young Icil-
      ius [1] pressed,
   And stamped his foot, and rent his gown, and
      smote upon his breast,
   And sprang upon that column,[2] by many a minstrel
      sung,
90 Whereon three mouldering helmets, three rusting
      swords, are hung,

---

[1] *Icilius.* One of the leaders of the Plebeians, who had been Tribune on two occasions, and who was betrothed to Virginia.

[2] *That column.* During the reign of Tullus Hostilius, the third
king of Rome, a dispute arose between the Latins and the Romans.
It was determined, in order to avoid a bloody battle in which many
would lose their lives, to decide the issue by a combat between the
three bravest warriors on either side. The choice of the Latins fell

And beckoned to the people, and in bold voice and
    clear,
Poured thick and fast the burning words which ty-
    rants quake to hear.

"Now, by your children's cradles, now by your
    fathers' graves,
Be men to-day, Quirites,[1] or be forever slaves!
95 For this did Servius[2] give us laws? For this did
    Lucrece bleed?[3]
For this was the great vengeance wrought on Tar-
    quin's evil seed?
For this did those false sons[4] make red the axes of
    their sire?

---

on three brothers named the Curiatii, and that of the Romans on three brothers named the Horatii. In the fight that followed, after two of the Horatii had fallen, the third brother, by pretending to run away, separated the Curiatii, who were all wounded, and returning killed his opponents in turn. The Romans, to commemorate this great victory, erected in the Forum a monument which they decorated with the swords and armor taken from the Curiatii.

[1] *Quirites.* "Originally the inhabitants of the Sabine town of Cures. After the Sabines and the Romans had united in one community, under Romulus, the name of *Quirites* was taken in addition to *Romani*, the Romans calling themselves in a civil capacity *Quirites*, while in a political and military capacity they retained the name *Romani*. It was a reproach for soldiers to be called Quirites." — ROLFE. See Note 3, page 93.

[2] *Servius.* The sixth king of Rome. He gave to the city a new constitution, by which the rights of the common people were protected, and he also made a fair division of the public lands. Servius was killed by Tarquin, his son-in-law, who seized the throne.

[3] *Lucrece bled.* See Introduction to *Horatius*, page 16.

[4] *False sons.* The two sons of Lucius Junius Brutus. See Introduction to *Horatius*, page 17.

For this did Scævola's right hand [1] hiss in the Tuscan fire?
Shall the vile fox-earth [2] awe the race that stormed the lion's den? [3]
100 Shall we, who could not brook one lord, crouch to the wicked Ten?
Oh for that ancient spirit which curbed the Senate's will!
Oh for the tents which in old time whitened the Sacred Hill! [4]
In those brave days our fathers stood firmly side by side;
They faced the Marcian fury; [5] they tamed the Fabian pride; [6]

---

[1] *Scævola's right hand.* After the destruction of the bridge over the Tiber, Lars Porsena with the Tuscan army besieged Rome. A brave Roman youth named Mucius resolved to free his country by killing Lars Porsena. He made his way into the camp of the enemy, and reached the royal tent, but by a mistake killed the secretary instead of the king. He was at once seised and threatened with being burned alive, unless he revealed the names of those who were concerned with him in the plot. To show his contempt for the threat, Mucius put his right hand in the flame of a fire, and held it there without flinching. Porsena was so much struck with the bravery of the youth that he pardoned him, and sent him back to Rome. The right hand Mucius had held in the fire was ever afterwards useless, so that he was known as *Scævola*, or "the left-handed."

[2] *Fox-earth.* The fox's hole.

[3] *Lion's den.* Shall we, who drove out Tarquin the Proud, tremble before Appius Claudius?

[4] *Sacred Hill.* See Note 2, page 54.

105 They drove the fiercest Quinctius [1] an outcas[t]
   from Rome;
They sent the haughtiest Claudius [2] with [his]
   fasces home.
But what their care bequeathed us our ma[d]
   flung away:
All the ripe fruit of threescore years was bli[ghted]
   in a day.
Exult, ye proud Patricians! The hard-fought [fight]
   is o'er.
110 We strove for honors [3] — 'twas in vain; for [free]-
   dom — 'tis no more.
No crier [4] to the polling summons the eager thro[ng]

---

victorious and ravaged the Roman territory, but in every cas[e]
spared the property of the Patricians, destroying only that of [the]
Plebeians. The ruin of the city seemed certain, but Coriolanus
finally persuaded to abandon his purpose by the pleadings of [his]
mother and his wife. He gave up the siege, and was put to death [by]
the Volscians.

  Fabian pride. It is said that on one occasion, when the Ro[man]
army under the Consul Cæso Fabius had defeated the people of V[eii]
the Plebeian infantry refused to attack the camp of the enemy [so]
that Fabius might be deprived of a complete victory, and, therefor[e,]
a triumph. See Note 4, page 101.

  [1] *Fiercest Quinctius.* Cæso Quinctius, son of the famous Dict[ator]
Cincinnatus, was a constant opponent of the Plebeians. He [was]
accused of having slain a man during a fight between the factio[ns at]
Rome, and was driven into exile, where he died.

  [2] *Haughtiest Claudius.* Flather says that the reference here i[s to]
Appius Claudius, the father of the Decemvir, who attempted to ma[ke a]
citizen who had been a commander of a company

No Tribune breathes the word of might that guards
    the weak from wrong.
Our very hearts, that were so high, sink down be-
    neath your will.
Riches, and lands, and power, and state — ye have
    them : — keep them still.
115 Still keep the holy fillets;[1] still keep the purple
    gown,[2]
The axes, and the curule chair,[3] the car, and laurel
    crown :[4]
Still press us for your cohorts,[5] and, when the fight
    is done,
Still fill your garners from the soil[6] which our good
    swords have won.
Still, like a spreading ulcer, which leech-craft[7] may
    not cure,

---

[1] *Holy fillets.* The fillets were head-bands worn by the priests as a sign of their office. Only Patricians were allowed to be priests.

[2] *Purple gown.* The gowns, or togas, worn by the chief magistrates had a broad purple border.

[3] *Curule chair.* See Note 1, page 82.

[4] *Car and laurel crown.* When a Roman general had won a complete victory over the enemy, he was granted a *triumph*. He rode, crowned with a laurel wreath, in a four-horse chariot, through the streets of the city, preceded by the spoils and the captives taken in the war and followed by his victorious troops. When he reached the temple of Jupiter on the Capitoline Hill, he dismounted and there sacrificed a white bull on the altar of the god. See *The Prophecy of Capys*, lines 233–268.

[5] *Cohorts.* The tenth part of a Roman legion; each cohort consisted of six companies, but the number of men in a company varied at different times. See Note 4, page 112.

[6] *From the soil.* One of the chief causes of difference between the Patricians and the Plebeians was the unfair distribution of the public lands. See Introduction, page 87.

[7] *Leech-craft.* The skill of a doctor.

>   But, by the Shades [4] beneath us, and by the gods
>   above,
>   Add not unto your cruel hate your yet more cruel
>   love!
>   Have ye not graceful ladies, whose spotless lineage
>   springs
> 130 From Consuls, and High Pontiffs, and ancient Alban kings? [5]
>   Ladies, who deign not on our paths to set their tender feet,
>   Who from their cars look down with scorn upon
>   the wondering street,

---

[1] *Foul usance.* The Plebeians complained bitterly of the high rate of interest charged by the wealthy Patricians on the money loaned to the poorer people. See Introduction, page 87.

[2] *Dog-star heat.* In midsummer, when Sirius, known as the dog-star, rose at about the same time as the sun.

[3] *Holes.* The stocks, in which the feet were confined.

[4] *Shades.* The spirits of the dead, who inhabited Hades, or the world after death.

[5] *Alban kings.* See Introduction to *The Prophecy of Capys*, page 117.

Who in Corinthian mirrors[1] their own proud smiles behold,
And breathe of Capuan odors,[2] and shine with Spanish gold?
135 Then leave the poor Plebeian his single tie to life —
The sweet, sweet love of daughter, of sister, and of wife,
The gentle speech, the balm for all that his vexed soul endures,
The kiss, in which he half forgets even such a yoke as yours.
Still let the maiden's beauty swell the father's breast with pride;
140 Still let the bridegroom's arms infold an unpolluted bride.
Spare us the inexpiable wrong, the unutterable shame,
That turns the coward's heart to steel, the sluggard's blood to flame,
Lest, when our latest hope is fled, ye taste of our despair,
And learn by proof, in some wild hour, how much the wretched dare."

. . . .
. . . .

145 Straightway[3] Virginius led the maid a little space aside,

---

[1] *Corinthian mirrors.* Polished bronze mirrors for the making of which Corinth was specially noted.

[2] *Capuan odors.* See Note 2, page 77.

[3] *Straightway.* It is understood, of course, that Appius Claudius, as the judge in the cause, has decided in favor of Marcus, and has given Virginia to him as his slave.

To where the reeking shambles [1] stood, piled up with
    horn and hide,
Close to yon low dark archway, where, in a crim-
    son flood,
Leaps down to the great sewer [2] the gurgling stream
    of blood.
Hard by, a flesher on a block had laid his whittle [3]
    down;
150 Virginius caught the whittle up, and hid it in his gown.
And then his eyes grew very dim, and his throat
    began to swell,
And in a hoarse, changed voice he spake, "Fare-
    well, sweet child! Farewell!
Oh, how I loved my darling! Though stern I
    sometimes be,
To thee, thou know'st I was not so. Who could be
    so to thee?
155 And how my darling loved me! How glad she
    was to hear
My footstep on the threshold when I came back
    last year!
And how she danced with pleasure to see my civic
    crown,[4]
And took my sword, and hung it up, and brought
    me forth my gown!

---

[1] *Shambles.* Slaughter-house.

[2] *Great sewer.* The *Cloaca Maxima,* or Great Drain of Rome, said to have been built by one of the early kings. It has been in existence for over twenty-five hundred years, and is still well preserved. See Map, page 6.

[3] *Whittle.* Knife.

[4] *Civic crown.* A crown of oak leaves, the highest award given to a Roman soldier. To wear the crown a soldier must have saved the life of a fellow-citizen in battle, slain his enemy, and held his ground after the combat.

The house that was the happiest within the Roman
    walls,
The house that envied not the wealth of Capua's
    marble halls,
165 Now, for the brightness of thy smile, must have
    eternal gloom,
And for the music of thy voice, the silence of the
    tomb.
The time is come. See how he points his eager
    hand this way!
See how his eyes gloat on thy grief, like a kite's
    upon the prey!
With all his wit, he little deems that, spurned, be-
    trayed, bereft,
170 Thy father hath in his despair one fearful refuge left.
He little deems that in this hand I clutch what still
    can save
Thy gentle youth from taunts and blows, the por-
    tion of the slave;
Yea, and from nameless evil, that passeth taunt
    and blow, —
Foul outrage which thou knowest not, which thou
    shalt never know.
175 Then clasp me round the neck once more, and give
    me one more kiss;
And now, mine own dear little girl, there is no way
    but this."

With that he lifted high the steel, and smote her
  the side,
And in her blood she sank to earth, and with on
  sob she died.

    Then, for a little moment, all people held their
  breath;
180 And through the crowded Forum was stillness as
  of death;
And in another moment brake forth from one
  and all
A cry as if the Volscians were coming o'er the
  wall.
Some with averted faces shrieking fled home
  amain;
Some ran to call a leech; and some ran to lift the
  slain;
185 Some felt her lips and little wrist, if life might
  there be found;
And some tore up their garments fast, and strove
  to stanch the wound.
In vain they ran, and felt, and stanched, for never
  truer blow
That good right arm had dealt in fight against a
  Volscian foe.

    When Appius Claudius saw that deed, he shud-
  dered and sank down,
190 And hid his face some little space with the corner
  of his gown,
Till, with white lips and bloodshot eyes, Virginius
  tottered nigh,

"O dwellers in the nether gloom,[1] avengers of the
   slain,
By this dear blood I cry to you, do right between
   us twain;
195 And even as Appius Claudius hath dealt by me
   and mine,
Deal you by Appius Claudius and all the Claudian
   line!"
So spake the slayer of his child, and turned, and
   went his way;
But first he cast one haggard glance to where the
   body lay,
And writhed, and groaned a fearful groan, and
   then, with steadfast feet,
200 Strode right across the market-place unto the Sacred Street.

Then up sprang Appius Claudius: "Stop him,
   alive or dead!
Ten thousand pounds of copper[2] to the man who
   brings his head!"
He looked upon his clients; but none would work
   his will.
He looked upon his lictors; but they trembled and
   stood still.
205 And, as Virginius through the press his way in
   silence cleft,
Ever the mighty multitude fell back to right and
   left.
And he hath passed in safety unto his woeful home,
And there ta'en horse to tell the camp what deeds
   are done in Rome.

By this the flood of people was
 every side,
210 And streets and porches round were
 that o'erflowing tide;
And close around the body gathered a littl
Of them that were the nearest and de
 slain.
They brought a bier, and hung it with
 cypress crown,[1]
And gently they uplifted her, and gently
 down.
215 The face of Appius Claudius wore the
 scowl and sneer,
And in the Claudian note he cried, "Wh
 this rabble here?
Have they no crafts to mind at home, that
 ward they stray?
Ho! lictors, clear the market-place, and fe
 corpse away!"
The voice of grief and fury till then had n
 loud;
220 But a deep sullen murmur wandered amo
 crowd,
Like the moaning noise that goes before the
 wind on the deep,
Or the growl of a fierce watch-dog but half
 from sleep.
But when the lictors at that word, tall yeo
 and strong,
Each with his axe and sheaf of twigs, wen
 into the throng.

The wailing, hooting, cursing, the howls of grief
    and hate,
Were heard beyond the Pincian Hill,[1] beyond the
    Latin Gate.[2]
But close around the body, where stood the little train
230 Of them that were the nearest and dearest to the
    slain,
No cries were there, but teeth set fast, low whispers and black frowns,
And breaking up of benches, and girding up of
    gowns;
'Twas well the lictors might not pierce to where
    the maiden lay,
Else surely had they been all twelve torn limb from
    limb that day.
235 Right glad they were to struggle back, blood streaming from their heads,
With axes all in splinters, and raiment all in shreds.
Then Appius Claudius gnawed his lip and the
    blood left his cheek;
And thrice he beckoned with his hand, and thrice
    he strove to speak;
And thrice the tossing Forum set up a frightful
    yell:
240 "See, see, thou dog! what thou hast done; and
    hide thy shame in hell!
Thou that wouldst make our maidens slaves must
    first make slaves of men.
Tribunes! Hurrah for Tribunes! Down with the
    wicked Ten!"
And straightway, thick as hailstones, came whizzing through the air

Pebbles, and bricks, and potsherds,[1] all round
    curule chair;
245 And upon Appius Claudius great fear and trembling came;
For never was a Claudius yet brave against aug
    but shame.
Though the great houses love us not, we own,
    do them right,
That the great houses, all save one, have born
    them well in fight.
Still Caius of Corioli,[2] his triumphs and his wrongs
250 His vengeance and his mercy, live in our camp-fire
    songs.
Beneath the yoke of Furius[3] oft have Gaul and
    Tuscan bowed;
And Rome may bear the pride of him of whom
    herself is proud.
But evermore a Claudius shrinks from a stricken
    field,[4]
And changes color like a maid at sight of sword
    and shield.
255 The Claudian triumphs all were won within the
    city towers;
The Claudian yoke was never pressed on any necks
    but ours.

---

[1] *Potsherds.* Pieces of broken pottery.

[2] *Caius of Corioli.* See Note 5, page 99.

[3] *Furius.* Marcus Furius Camillus defeated the Gauls after they had captured Rome in 390 B.C. He is also said to have captured the Etruscan city of Veii. He was the leader of the Patrician party in Rome, and a strong opponent of the demands of the common people. See Note 2, page 34.

[4] *Stricken field.* A fiercely contested battle, the issue of which is doubtful.

A Cossus,[1] like a wild-cat, springs ever at the face;
A Fabius[2] rushes like a boar against the shouting chase;
But the vile Claudian litter, raging with currish spite,
260 Still yelps and snaps at those who run, still runs from those who smite.
So now 'twas seen of Appius. When stones began to fly,
He shook, and crouched, and wrung his hands, and smote upon his thigh.
"Kind clients, honest lictors, stand by me in this fray!
Must I be torn in pieces? Home, home, the nearest way!"
265 While yet he spake, and looked around with a bewildered stare,
Four sturdy lictors put their necks beneath the curule chair;
And fourscore clients on the left, and fourscore on the right,
Arrayed themselves with swords and staves, and loins girt up for fight.
But, though without or staff or sword, so furious was the throng,
270 That scarce the train with might and main could bring their lord along.

---

[1] *Cossus.* One of the most famous members of the Cossus family was Servius Cornelius Cossus, who, during a battle with the people of Veii, killed the king of that city in single combat. This was considered the greatest deed that a general could perform, and was repeated on only two other occasions in Roman history. See Note 2, page 72.

[2] *Fabius.* "The Fabian race was one of the most ancient Patrician families at Rome, tracing its origin to Hercules. The family was celebrated in early Roman history. Being looked on with disfavor by their own order, they offered to carry on the war against

him down.
And sharper came the pelting; and evermore th[e]
yell —
"Tribunes! we will have Tribunes!" rose with [a]
louder swell.
275 And the chair tossed as tosses a bark with tattered sail
When raves the Adriatic[1] beneath an eastern gale,
When the Calabrian sea-marks[2] are lost in clouds of spume,
And the great Thunder Cape[3] has donned his veil of inky gloom.
One stone hit Appius in the mouth, and one beneath the ear;
280 And ere he reached Mount Palatine, he swooned with pain and fear.

Veii at their own cost and alone. When the offer was joyfully accepted, three hundred and six Fabii marched forth, under the lead of Cæso Fabius, to the banks of the Cremera, where they erected a fortress. After carrying on the war successfully for a time, they were enticed into an ambuscade, and the whole race perished except one bo[y] who had been left at Rome on account of his youth." — ROLFE. See *The Battle of the Lake Regillus*, lines 693-694.

[1] *The Adriatic.* Sailors held in dread the navigation of the Adriatic Sea, on account of the sudden violent storms to which it was subject.

[2] *Calabrian sea-marks.* Either the headlands of the Calabrian coasts or the lighthouses on these headlands. *Spume* is foam.

[3] *Thunder Cape.* Acroceraunia, a very rocky mountain on the west coast of Greece, extending into the sea. It is said to have received its name on account of the many thunder-storms that occur there.

God send Rome one such other sight, and send me
there to see!

. . . .

---

[1] *Grandson.* Appius Claudius Crassus, the opponent of the Tribunes Licinius and Sextius. See Introduction, page 89.

ADRIAT
SEA

Beneventum
CAMP
Pæstum

TYRRHENIAN

SEA
Croton

Syracuse   SCALE OF MILES

The Romans were defeated at the battles of Heraclea and
but were victorious in the final battle at Beneventum.

INTRODUCTION TO
THE PROPHECY OF CAPYS

In 280 B.C. a war broke out between Rome and Tarentum, one of the Greek cities on the Bay of Tarentum in southern Italy. The Tarentines were jealous of the increase of Roman power, and when a Roman fleet anchored in the Bay of Tarentum, contrary to an existing treaty, they attacked it, sinking some of the ships and killing the commander. The Romans demanded satisfaction for the injury, but their ambassadors were openly insulted by the Tarentines in the theatre of the city. War followed. The Tarentines knew that alone they were no match for the Romans, so they called on Pyrrhus, king of Epirus, to aid them in their struggle. Pyrrhus, who was anxious to win an empire in the west and to be known as a great conqueror, was quite ready to help, and landed in Italy with twenty thousand foot-soldiers, five thousand cavalry, and twenty elephants.

The first battle was fought at Heraclea, and Pyrrhus gained a complete victory over the Roman legions. The Romans, fighting on a level plain, could make no impression on the Greeks, drawn up in solid masses, sixteen men deep, with their shields almost locked, and their long spears projecting in front. The horses of the Roman cavalry, also, were so frightened at the sight of the elephants, and their trumpeting, that they ran away, thus carrying confusion into their own ranks. In the next year another battle, very similar to that at Heraclea, was fought at Asculum, and the Romans were again defeated. But these two victories were so dearly bought that Pyrrhus was ready for peace on almost any terms.

Pyrrhus now spent nearly three years in Sicily, returning to Italy in 276 B.C., when the war with Rome was continued. But conditions had entirely changed. The Romans had learned wisdom from their former reverses, and moreover they were under the command of an able soldier, the Consul Manius Curius Dentatus. This time the battle was fought at Beneventum, among the mountains, where the Greeks were at a disadvantage. Curius had instructed the archers to attach burning tow to their arrows and to shoot them among the elephants. This so frightened the beasts that they rushed through their own ranks, causing fearful slaughter. The victory of the Romans was overwhelming. Pyrrhus collected the remnants of his army, and set sail for Greece, leaving Tarentum to its fate.

ROMAN SOLDIER WITH FULL ARMOR

"The conquerors," says Macaulay, "had a good right to exult in their success. They had not learned from their enemy how to conquer him. It was with their own national arms, and in their own national battle array, that they had overcome weapons and tactics long believed to be invincible. The pilum and the broadsword had vanquished the Macedonian spear. The legion had broken the Macedonian phalan Even the elephants, when the surprise produced by their first appearance was over, could cause no disorder in the steady, yet flexible, battalions of Rome." Such a glorious victory would be likely to excite the strongest feelings of national pride and to call forth songs of triumph of which the past and future glories of the city would form the theme. Such a song is *The Prophecy of Capys*, which deals with the marvellous story of the foundation of the city, and prophesies its future greatness.

The story of the foundation of Rome may be told very briefly.

The Romans trace their descent to Ascanius, the son of Æneas, the Trojan hero, who, after the fall of Troy, took refuge in Italy and settled among the Latins. Æneas married Lavinia, the daughter of Latinus, the king of the country, and founded a city which he named Lavinium in her honor. After the death of Æneas, Ascanius removed from Lavinium, and founded Alba Longa, the "Long White City," on a spur of the Alban Hills, about fifteen miles south-east of the site of Rome. Ascanius was succeeded by Sylvius, and after him eleven kings of the "great Sylvian line" ruled over Alba Longa. Procras, the last of these kings, left two sons. The younger, Amulius, seized the crown which rightfully belonged to his elder brother Numitor, who was a quiet, unambitious man, content to dwell among his flocks and his herds. But Numitor had two children, a son and a daughter, and Amulius, in order to avoid future trouble, put the son to death, and compelled the daughter, Rhea Sylvia, to become a Vestal Virgin. The god Mars, however, fell in love with Rhea Sylvia, and she became the mother of twin boys. As soon as Amulius heard of this he condemned the mother to be buried alive, and ordered the two boys to be thrown into the Tiber.

In accordance with the cruel order of Amulius, the twins were placed in a basket, and set adrift on the river. But the frail boat was driven ashore in shallow water, which shrank and left the children lying on dry land. Here they were found by a she-wolf, who nursed them, until they were discovered by Faustulus, a herdsman of Amulius, who took them home, named them Romulus and Remus, and brought them up as his own sons.

When they grew to man's estate, Romulus and Remus were noted for their personal beauty and their daring spirit. They helped Faustulus to attend to the king's herds, and, one day in a conflict with the herdsmen of Numitor, Remus was taken prisoner. When he saw him, Numitor suspected him to be his grandson, and this suspicion was confirmed, when Romulus, who had come to ransom his brother, appeared. The youths were acknowledged by their grandfather and told their history. They at once called together their friends and the adherents of their grandfather, and attacked Amulius in his palace. The usurper was killed and Numitor placed in possession of the throne of which he had been unjustly deprived.

After a time Romulus and Remus resolved to leave Alba Longa, and to found a city o

A ROMAN SACRIFICE

wished the city to bear his name and to build it on the Aventine Hill. Finally, they agreed to leave the decision to the will of the gods, as expressed by the flight of birds. Remus, standing on the Aventine, saw six vultures in full flight, but just as he reached Romulus, who had taken his stand on the Palatine, to tell him of his good fortune, twelve vultures appeared also in full flight. The dispute again arose; Remus had seen the first flight, but twice as many birds were seen by Romulus. As it was impossible to come to an agreement, the brothers separated and Romulus proceeded to build his city alone.

Romulus first erected a low wall around the site of the proposed city to mark the boundary and as a protection against invaders. One day Remus appeared, and in derision jumped over the low wall. Romulus, carried away by rage, seized a spade, and killed his brother, crying out, "So perish any one who shall hereafter attempt to leap over my wall." Such is the story of the founding of the city of Rome in the year 753 B.C.

Professor Morey gives the following description of the Roman method of fighting in use during the war with Pyrrhus: "When drawn up in order of battle, the legion was arranged in three lines: first, the young men; second, the more experienced soldiers; third, the veterans, capable of supporting the other two lines. Each line was composed of ten companies, those of the first two lines consisting of one hundred and twenty men each, and those of the third line consisting of sixty men each; the companies in each line were so arranged that they were opposite the spaces in the next line. This arrangement enabled the companies in front to retreat into the spaces in the rear, or the companies in the rear to advance to the spaces in front. Behind the third line usually fought the light-armed and less experienced soldiers. The defensive armor of all the three lines was alike—a coat of mail for the breast, a brass helmet for the head, greaves for the legs, and a large oblong shield carried upon the left arm. For offensive weapons, each man carried a short sword, which could be used for cutting or thrusting. The soldiers in the first two lines each had also two javelins, to be hurled at the enemy before coming into close quarters; and those of the third line each had a long lance, which could be used for piercing. It was with such arms as these that the Roman soldiers conquered Italy."

THE PROPHECY OF CAPYS

A LAY SUNG AT THE BANQUET IN THE CAPITOL, ON THE DAY WHEREON MANIUS CURIUS DENTATUS, A SECOND TIME CONSUL, TRIUMPHED OVER KING PYRRHUS AND THE TARENTINES, IN THE YEAR OF THE CITY [1] CCCCLXXIX

1

Now slain is King Amulius,[2]
   Of the great Sylvian line,[3]
Who reigned in Alba Longa,
   On the throne of Aventine.[4]
5   Slain is the Pontiff Camers,
   Who spake the words of doom:
"The children to the Tiber;
   The mother to the tomb."[5]

2

In Alba's lake [6] no fisher

On the dark rind of Alba's oaks
  To-day no axe is ringing:
The yoke hangs o'er the manger:
  The scythe lies in the hay:
Through all the Alban villages
  No work is done to-day.

3

And every Alban burgher
  Hath donned his whitest gown;
And every head in Alba
  Weareth a poplar crown;[1]
And every Alban door-post
  With boughs and flowers is gay:
For to-day the dead are living;
  The lost are found to-day.

4

They were doomed by a bloody king:
  They were doomed by a lying priest:
They were cast on the raging flood:
  They were tracked by the raging beast:
Raging beast and raging flood
  Alike have spared the prey;
And to-day the dead are living;
  The lost are found to-day.

---

being surrounded on all sides by steep banks, some of which rise to a height of two or three hundred feet above the level of the lake. It is undoubtedly the crater of an extinct volcano. It is 918 feet above the sea level, and its waters are of great depth." — ROLFE.

[1] *Poplar crown.* As the poplar was sacred to the Greek hero, Hercules, who became famous as the destroyer of monsters, it was fitting that leaves of that tree should be worn in celebrating the death of the tyrant Amulius.

5

The troubled river knew them,
  And smoothed his yellow foam,
And gently rocked the cradle
  That bore the fate of Rome.
The ravening she-wolf knew them,
  And lick'd them o'er and o'er,
And gave them of her own fierce milk,
  Rich with raw flesh and gore.
Twenty winters, twenty springs,
  Since then have rolled away;
And to-day the dead are living:
  The lost are found to-day.

6

Blithe it was to see the twins,
  Right goodly youths and tall,
Marching from Alba Longa
  To their old grandsire's hall.
Along their path fresh garlands
  Are hung from tree to tree;
Before them stride the pipers,
  Piping a note of glee.

7

On the right goes Romulus,
  With arms to the elbows red,
And in his hand a broadsword,
  And on the blade a head —
A head in an iron helmet,
  With horse-hair hanging down,
A shaggy head, a swarthy head,
  Fixed in a ghastly frown —
The head of King Amulius
  Of the great Sylvian line,

Who reigned in Alba Longa,
   On the throne of Aventine.

8

On the left side goes Remus,
   With wrists and fingers red,
And in his hand a boar-spear,
   And on the point a head —
A wrinkled head and aged,
   With silver beard and hair,
And holy fillets [1] round it,
   Such as the pontiffs wear —
The head of ancient Camers,
   Who spake the words of doom:
"The children to the Tiber;
   The mother to the tomb."

9

Two and two behind the twins
   Their trusty comrades go,
Four and forty valiant men,
   With club, and axe, and bow.
On each side every hamlet
   Pours forth its joyous crowd,
Shouting lads and baying dogs
   And children laughing loud,
And old men weeping fondly
   As Rhea's boys [2] go by,
And maids who shriek to see the heads,
   Yet, shrieking, press more nigh.

10

So they marched along the lake;
   They marched by fold and stall,

---

[1] *Holy fillets.* See Note 1, page 101.
[2] *Rhea's boys.* The children of Rhea Sylvia.

By cornfield and by vineyard,
    Unto the old man's hall.

11

In the hall-gate sate Capys,
    Capys, the sightless seer;[1]
From head to foot he trembled
    As Romulus drew near.
And up stood stiff his thin white hair,
    And his blind eyes flashed fire:
"Hail! foster-child of the wondrous nurse!
    Hail! son of the wondrous sire!

12

"But thou — what dost thou here
    In the old man's peaceful hall?
What doth the eagle in the coop,
    The bison in the stall?
Our corn fills many a garner;
    Our vines clasp many a tree;
Our flocks are white on many a hill;
    But these are not for thee.

13

"For thee no treasure ripens
    In the Tartessian mine:[2]
For thee no ship brings precious bales
    Across the Libyan brine:[3]

    Thou shalt not drink from amber;[1]
        Thou shalt not rest on down;
115 Arabia shall not steep thy locks,[2]
        Nor Sidon tinge thy gown.[3]

14

"Leave gold and myrrh and jewels,
    Rich table and soft bed,
To them who of man's seed are born,
120   Whom woman's milk have fed.
Thou wast not made for lucre,[4]
    For pleasure, nor for rest;
Thou, that art sprung from the War-god's loins,
    And hast tugged at the she-wolf's breast.

15

125 "From sunrise unto sunset
    All earth shall hear thy fame:
A glorious city thou shalt build,
    And name it by thy name:
And there, unquenched through ages,
130   Like Vesta's sacred fire,[5]
Shall live the spirit of thy nurse,
    The spirit of thy sire.

---

[1] *From amber.* From a cup of amber.

[2] *Steep thy locks.* Thou shalt not steep thy hair in the perfumes of Arabia.

16

 "The ox toils through the furrow,
  Obedient to the goad;
135 The patient ass, up flinty paths,
  Plods with his weary load:
 With whine and bound the spaniel
  His master's whistle hears;
 And the sheep yields her patiently
140 To the loud clashing shears.

17

 "But thy nurse will hear no master;
  Thy nurse will bear no load;
 And woe to them that shear her,
  And woe to them that goad!
145 When all the pack, loud baying,
  Her bloody lair surrounds,
 She dies in silence, biting hard,
  Amidst the dying hounds.

18

 "Pomona[1] loves the orchard;
150 And Liber[2] loves the vine;
 And Pales[3] loves the straw-built shed
  Warm with the breath of kine;

---

[1] *Pomona.* The goddess of fruits and gardens. The Romans erected a temple in her honor, over which a special priest presided, who offered sacrifices for the preservation of the fruits.

[2] *Liber.* An ancient Roman divinity, usually considered the same as Bacchus, the god of wine. A festival was held each year in his honor at Rome, on the 17th of March.

[3] *Pales.* The goddess of flocks and shepherds, one of the most ancient of the Roman divinities. Her festival was also celebrated annually at Rome.

And Venus [1] loves the whispers
  Of plighted youth and maid,
155 In April's ivory moonlight
  Beneath the chestnut shade.

19

"But thy father loves the clashing
  Of broadsword and of shield :
He loves to drink the steam that reeks
160 From the fresh battle-field :
He smiles a smile more dreadful
  Than his own dreadful frown,
When he sees the thick black cloud of smoke
  Go up from the conquered town.

20

165 "And such as is the War-god,
  The author of thy line,
And such as she who suckled thee,
  Even such be thou and thine.
Leave to the soft Campanian [2]
170 His baths and his perfumes ;
Leave to the sordid race of Tyre
  Their dyeing-vats and looms :
Leave to the sons of Carthage
  The rudder and the oar :
175 Leave to the Greek his marble Nymphs [3]
  And scrolls [4] of wordy lore.

---

[1] *Venus.* The goddess of love and beauty. Venus was the mother of Æneas, the great ancestor of the Romans.

[2] *Soft Campanian.* See Note 2, page 77.

[3] *Nymphs.* The Nymphs were regarded as divine, and were supposed to preside over streams, mountains, trees, etc.

[4] *Scrolls.* Rolls of papyrus or parchment.

21

"Thine, Roman, is the pilum:[1]
    Roman, the sword[2] is thine,
The even trench,[3] the bristling mound,[3]
    The legion's ordered line;[4]
And thine the wheels of triumph,[5]
    Which with their laurelled train
Move slowly up the shouting streets
    To Jove's eternal fane.[6]

22

"Beneath thy yoke the Volscian[7]
    Shall veil his lofty brow:
Soft Capua's curled revellers[8]
    Before thy chairs shall bow:

---

[1] *The pilum.* The Roman spear, nearly seven feet in length, which was used either to thrust with or to throw. The shaft was of wood, with a barbed iron head. See Illustration, page 116.

[2] *The sword.* The celebrated short sword of the Romans was only about two feet long, but was several inches wide. It was pointed at the end, and sharpened on both sides. See Illustration, page 116.

[3] *Trench ... mound.* Each Roman soldier carried, as part of his equipment, a spade and several stakes. When the camp was pitched, a trench was at once dug, and a mound thrown up and further defended with a line of stakes.

[4] *Ordered line.* The Roman legion at first consisted of three thousand infantry and three hundred cavalry. The number of the infantry was afterwards increased to six thousand.

[5] *Triumph.* See Note 4, page 101.

[6] *Jove's eternal fane.* The temple of Jupiter on the Capitoline Hill built by Tarquinius Superbus. See Map, page 6, and Introduction to *Horatius*, page 15. It was dedicated to Jupiter, Juno, and Minerva, but was known as the temple of Jupiter. Here the victorious general offered sacrifices to the gods. See Illustration, page 118.

[7] *The Volscian.* See Note 1, page 47.

[8] *Curled revellers.* See Note 2, page 77.

The Lucumoes of Arnus [1]
190   Shall quake thy rods to see;
And the proud Samnite's [2] heart of steel
    Shall yield to only thee.

23

"The Gaul [3] shall come against thee
    From the land of snow and night:
195 Thou shalt give his fair-haired armies
    To the raven and the kite.

24

"The Greek [4] shall come against thee,
    The conqueror of the East.
Beside him stalks to battle
200   The huge earth-shaking beast, [5]
The beast on whom the castle
    With all its guards doth stand,
The beast who hath between his eyes
    The serpent for a hand.

---

[1] *Lucumoes of Arnus.* The nobles of Etruria. The Arnus, now the Arno, was one of the rivers of Etruria. See Note 4, page 31.

[2] *Samnite.* The Samnites were a brave mountain race of central Italy. They waged three bitter wars with the Romans, in the second of which they inflicted upon them the most humiliating defeat in their history. They were conquered in the third war, but they afterwards joined with Pyrrhus against the Romans, again being defeated. See Frontispiece.

[3] *The Gaul.* The Gauls were among the most persistent and dangerous enemies of the Romans. On one occasion, in 390 B.C., they captured the city, and only through the bravery and skill of Camillus were they defeated. See Note 3, page 110.

[4] *The Greek.* Pyrrhus, king of Epirus. See Introduction, page 115.

[5] *Earth-shaking beast.* The elephant.

205   First march the bold Epirotes,[1]
         Wedged close with shield and spear;[2]
      And the ranks of false Tarentum
         Are glittering in the rear.

25

      "The ranks of false Tarentum
210   Like hunted sheep shall fly:
      In vain the bold Epirotes
         Shall round their standards die:
      And Apennine's gray vultures
         Shall have a noble feast
215   On the fat and the eyes
         Of the huge earth-shaking beast.

26

      "Hurrah! for the good weapons
         That keep the War-god's land.
      Hurrah! for Rome's stout pilum
220   In a stout Roman hand.
      Hurrah! for Rome's short broadsword,
         That through the thick array
      Of levelled spears and serried shields
         Hews deep its gory way.

27

225   "Hurrah! for the great triumph
         That stretches many a mile.
      Hurrah! for the wan captives
         That pass in endless file.

---

[1] *Epirotes.* The people of Epirus, one of the regions of northern

>   Ho! bold Epirotes, whither
> 230   Hath the Red King[1] ta'en flight?
>   Ho! dogs of false Tarentum,
>   Is not the gown washed white?[2]

28

> "Hurrah! for the great triumph
>   That stretches many a mile.
> 235 Hurrah! for the rich dye of Tyre,
>   And the fine web of Nile,[3]
> The helmets gay with plumage
>   Torn from the pheasant's wings,
> The belts set thick with starry gems
> 240   That shone on Indian kings,
> The urns of massy silver,
>   The goblets rough with gold,
> The many-colored tablets[4] bright
>   With loves and wars of old,
> 245 The stone[5] that breathes and struggles,
>   The brass[6] that seems to speak;—

---

[1] *Red King.* Pyrrhus in Greek means red or flame-colored.

[2] *Washed white.* When Lucius Posthumius was sent as ambassador to Tarentum, he was received by the whole people in the theatre of the city. He spoke to them in Greek, but he was so little acquainted with that language, that his address was received with shouts of laughter. He remonstrated, but was hissed from the stage. As he retired, a drunken buffoon ran up to him, and spattered his white robe with mud. Posthumius appealed to the people, but they only laughed at him and applauded his disgrace. "Men of Tarentum," said Posthumius, "it will take not a little blood to wash this gown."

[3] *Web of Nile.* Fabrics woven in Egypt.

[4] *Tablets.* Pictures.

[5] *Stone.* The marble statuary of the Greeks, so lifelike that it seemed to breathe and move.

[6] *Brass.* Bronze statues so natural that they seemed to speak.

Such cunning they who dwell on high
  Have given unto the Greek.

29

"Hurrah! for Manius Curius,[1]
  The bravest son of Rome,
Thrice in utmost need sent forth,
  Thrice drawn in triumph home.
Weave, weave for Manius Curius
  The third embroidered gown:[2]
Make ready the third lofty car,
  And twine the third green crown;
And yoke the steeds of Rosea[3]
  With necks like a bended bow,
And deck the bull, Mevania's[4] bull,
  The bull as white as snow.

30

"Blest and thrice blest the Roman
  Who sees Rome's brightest day,
Who sees that long victorious pomp
  Wind down the Sacred Way,
And through the bellowing Forum,
  And round the Suppliants' Grove,[5]

---

[1] *Manius Curius.* See Introduction, page 116.

[2] *Third embroidered gown.* The victorious general wore during the triumphal procession a gown embroidered with gold. This was the third triumph that had been granted to Manius Curius, the two others being on account of victories over the Sabines and Samnites.

[3] *Rosea.* A district in Italy celebrated for its horses.

[4] *Mevania.* A city in Umbria noted for its breed of white cattle. The bull was to be sacrificed to Jupiter when the procession reached the temple of the god.

WS - #0018 - 240823 - C0 - 229/152/8 [10] - CB - 9780331559101 - Gloss Lamination